The Iron Sceptre of the Son of Man

Os Justi Studies in Catholic Tradition

General Editor: Peter A. Kwasniewski

1 • J. Joy, *Disputed Questions on Papal Infallibility*

2 • R.-M. Rivoire, *Does "Traditionis Custodes" Pass the Juridical Rationality Test?*

3 • J. Shaw, *The Liturgy, the Family, and the Crisis of Modernity*

4 • P. Kwasniewski (ed.), *Illusions of Reform*

5 • G. Steckler, *The Triumph of Romanticism*

6 • T. Crean, *"Letters from that City . . .": A Guide to Holy Scripture for Students of Theology*

7 • S. Lanzetta, *God's Abode with Man: The Mystery of Divine Grace*

8 • A. Fimister, *The Iron Sceptre of the Son of Man*

The Iron Sceptre of the Son of Man

Romanitas as a Note of the Church

Alan Fimister

Lincoln, Nebraska

Os Justi Press
P.O. Box 21814
Lincoln, NE 68542
www.osjustipress.com

Send inquiries to
info@osjustipress.com

ISBN 978-1-960711-40-3 (paperback)
ISBN 978-1-960711-41-0 (hardcover)
ISBN 978-1-960711-42-7 (eBook)

Typesetting by Nora Malone
Cover design by Julian Kwasniewski
On the cover: Upper section of the sceptre of Charles V,
or "sceptre of Charlemagne" (before 1380).

To Fr Yosyp Veresh

and

Fr Thomas Crean O.P.

Τίνες Ῥωμαίοις Ῥωμαίων οἰκειότεροι σύμμαχοι[†]
Demetrios Kydones

[†] *Oratio pro subsidio latinorum* (PG 154:977D).

Contents

Acknowledgments

On the Feast of St Romanus 1987, I was baptised in a church whose high altar is built directly on top of the frontier of the Roman empire. The tabernacle of St Dominic's Priory Church stands immediately above Hadrian's Wall. My godfather is a Catholic of the Byzantine Rite, my godmother a Catholic of the Roman Rite. Later, when I served Mass at that altar, I could not but be struck by the momentous words of the priest immediately before he ascends the steps and (in that place) enters the Roman empire: *Judica me, Deus, et discerne causam meam de gente non sancta: ab homine iniquo et doloso eripe me.* I had known for as long as I could remember that my home town was a Roman city, and with every year of my life and study this fact has pleased me more.

The first time I visited the United States, where I have now lived for the last eight years, was for the wedding of a friend who then lived in Houston, Texas. He asked me if there was anything I would particularly like to see and I replied "the Spanish Governor's Palace in San Antonio." My absurdly generous friend volunteered to drive me there the day after (the wedding was not for another week) and I had the eccentric amusement of getting to see the westernmost public building on earth to bear the double-headed eagle of the Holy Roman Empire. Little did I know then that the next wedding I would attend in Texas would be my own.

The thought contained in this volume and good deal of the text were crystalized while I was teaching and studying far east along the *limes imperii* in the former diocese of St Methodius at the International Theological Institute between 2009 and 2014. During that time, I had the great honour of assisting in his labours Fr Yosyp Veresh, the Director of the Centre for Eastern Christian Studies, my next-door neighbour, mentor and friend. Those happy years were further enriched by the arrival of another mentor and friend, Fr Thomas Crean O.P., who was completing his doctoral studies on the Council of Florence. These two men have embodied for me the spirit of the Old and the New Rome. This period was crowned by my engagement and marriage to my dear wife Colleen, and, at the end of 2014, Fr Thomas graciously consented to officiate at our Nuptial Mass in Lufkin, Texas.

I will always be grateful to my two thesis examiners at the ITI: Dr Dagny Kjaergaard, author of all the best bits in the *Catechism of the Catholic Church* and living embodiment of the *sensus fidei*, and Dr William Newton, then the chair of the faculty at Steubenville's Austrian campus, my discussions with whom, when travelling between Trumau and Gaming, were always tremendously enlightening and improving. I must also remember Msgr. Larry Hogan, a chance reunion with whom in Norcia brought me back to Austria in 2009 and who would become the ITI's very own beloved *katechon*.

Thank you to Dr Bettina Tonn for her cartographical skills and for keeping me on track for two decades. You have a part stake in this enterprise, so I hope it is still to your liking. Thanks too to Joshua Charles for many long and fruitful discussions of the issues contained in this work.

Dr Peter Kwasniewski taught me long ago in Gaming when I was a lowly STM student and held my hand through the mysteries of the *via negativa*. I stand in awe of his ability to produce philosophical prose, theological broadsides, and major motets on a seemingly monthly basis while finding time to prod me into the long-delayed completion of the *Iron Sceptre* for Os Justi Press.

The thoughts born in those years have marinated for a long time and, I hope, matured. One of the things which has become much clearer to me than it was in 2014 is the greatness of the Byzantine centuries and the fidelity with which New Rome handed on the tradition it received, the great white horse of the Word of God without whose mighty example the lesser steeds that followed would surely have faltered.

Nor monkish order only
Slides down, as field to fen,
All things achieved and chosen pass,
As the White Horse fades in the grass,
No work of Christian men.

Preface

Moreover, the prince of the apostles still reigns and commands in the apostolic seat, and in the midst of it judicial rigour is established; and what remains for you is to unsheathe against evildoers, father, the sword of Peter, which he set for this purpose over nations and kingdoms. The cross of Christ preceded the eagles of Caesar, the sword of Peter before the sword of Constantine, and the judgement of the apostolic see takes precedence over that of the imperial power. Is your power from God or from men? Did not the God of gods speak to you in the apostle Peter, saying: "Whatsoever you bind on earth shall be bound in heaven; and whatever you loose on earth shall be loosed in heaven?" (Matthew 16). Why, then, all this time do you so negligently, nay, so cruelly, delay, or rather not dare, to release my son? But you will say that this power was entrusted to you over souls, not bodies. Be it so. It is certainly enough for us if you bind the souls of those who keep my son bound in prison; it is easy for you to release my son, provided that the fear of God takes away the human fear. Therefore, give me back my son, man of God, if you are a man of God, and not rather a man of blood, as you will be if you hesitate in the deliverance of my son, so that the Most High may require his blood at your hand (Gen. 9). Alas, alas, if the chief shepherd should turn into a mercenary, if he should flee from the face of the wolf, if he should leave the lamb entrusted to

> him, or rather the chosen ram, the leader of the Lord's flock, in the jaws of the bloody beast![1]

In the early church, when a bishop died the faithful in good standing, those permitted to attend the Mass of the Faithful and receive communion, would gather to elect a new bishop. At the same time the clergy, the deacons, the presbyters and the Metropolitan or suffragans (depending if the late prelate was himself a suffragan or a Metropolitan) would also gather. A race to the finish would then ensue, one of the two groups either clerical or lay would reach a consensus first as to who the new bishop should be and then the other would have to decide whether or not to acquiesce. Usually, but not always, it would be the clergy, and the assembled people would respond to their nomination with cries either of Axios! (worthy) or Anaxios! (unworthy).

The bishop himself, of course, controlled who counted as one of the faithful, imposing and lifting excommunications for moral and doctrinal

[1] Eleanor of Aquitaine to Celestine III on his failure to excommunicate the emperor Henry VI for imprisoning her son Richard I the Lionheart on his way home from the Third Crusade. "Porro princeps apostolorum adhuc in apostolica sede regnat et imperat, et in medio constitutus est judiciarius rigor; illudque restat, ut exeratis in maleficos, Pater, gladium Petri, quem ad hoc constituit super gentes et regna. Christi crux antecessit Caesaris aquilas, gladius Petri gladio Constantini, et apostolica sedes praejudicat imperatoriae potestati. Vestra potestas a Deo est, an ab hominibus? Nonne Deus deorum locutus est vobis in Petro apostolo dicens: 'Quodcunque ligaveris super terram, erit ligatum et in coelis; et quodcunque solveris super terram, erit solutum et in coelis?' (Matth. XVI). Quare ergo tanto tempore tam negligenter, imo tam crudeliter filium meum solvere differtis, aut potius non audetis? Sed dicetis hanc potestatem vobis in animabus, non in corporibus fuisse commissam. Esto: certe sufficit nobis, si eorum ligaveritis animas, qui filium meum ligatum in carcere tenent; filium meum solvere, vobis in expedito est, dummodo humanum timorem Dei timor evacuet. Redde igitur mihi filium meum, vir Dei, si tamen vir Dei es, et non potius vir sanguinum, si in filii mei liberatione torpeas, ut sanguinem ejus de manu tua requirat Altissimus (Gen. IX). Heu, heu, si summus pastor in mercenarium pervertatur, si a facie lupi fugiat, si commissam sibi oviculam imo arietem electum, ducem Dominici gregis, in faucibus cruentae bestiae derelinquat!" (PL 206:1270).

aberrations. He also appointed and ordained all the lower clergy. He thereby determined the shape of the electorate that would choose his successor.

This procedure strikingly reflects the mechanism for electing the emperor himself. Until the death of Augustus in AD 14, the Assembly of the Roman People continued to elect the magistrates and (with the Senate) enact the highest form of Roman Law: the *Lex*. After the accession of Tiberius, the Assembly met only at the beginning of each imperial reign when it would enact a *Lex de Imperio* by which the powers of the Republic were placed for his lifetime into the hands of the *Princeps Imperator*. Instead of being made up of the officials and former officials elected by the people, the Senate was henceforth made up of the officials and former officials appointed by the emperor, retaining in theory significant legislative power.[2]

Today the title "emperor" seems much grander and more impressive than the humble title of "king," but it was not ever thus. The title emperor or *imperator* and the official title of the Roman emperor, Augustus (such as is, for example, used in Acts 25:21 and 25), were both adopted in order to avoid the more exalted title of king.[3] After the deposition of the last Roman king Tarquinius Superbus in 509 BC[4] the title of king became hateful to the Roman People.[5] Gaius Julius Caesar, the great uncle of the

2 See *Codex Justinianus* 1.14.8: "Humanum esse probamus, si quid de cetero in publica vel in privata causa emerserit necessarium, quod formam generalem et antiquis legibus non insertam exposcat, id ab omnibus antea tam proceribus nostri palatii quam gloriosissimo coetu vestro, patres conscripti, tractari et, si universis tam iudicibus quam vobis placuerit, tunc allegata dictari et sic ea denuo collectis omnibus recenseri et, cum omnes consenserint, tunc demum in sacro nostri numinis consistorio recitari, ut universorum consensus nostrae serenitatis auctoritate firmetur."

3 Although St Bede is not happy even with the title *Augustus*. See St Bede, *Commentary on Revelation*, trans. F. Wallis (Liverpool: Liverpool University Press, 2013), 198.

4 This is a traditional date. Precision and certainty are not on offer at this period.

5 Andrew Erskine, "Hellenistic Monarchy and Roman Political Invective," *The Classical Quarterly* New Series, vol. 41, no. 1 (1991): 112. "Iis enim regiis quadraginta annis et ducentis paulo cum interregnis fere amplius praeteritis expulsoque Tarquinio tantum

first emperor, was assassinated precisely because he was suspected of a desire to make himself king.[6] Octavian, the first emperor, did not dare to adopt the title himself even when he enjoyed unchallenged command of the Roman world after the Battle of Actium in 31 BC.[7] Indeed, Octavian, renamed Augustus by the Senate in 27 BC in an act seen as the foundational moment of the empire, made a virtue of his eschewal of the title of king. He characterised his adoption of the name Augustus, a moment seen by historians since the Renaissance as the end of the Republic, as its restoration. As he records in his *Res Gestae*:

> In my sixth and seventh consulates, after putting out the civil war, having obtained all things by universal consent, I handed over the Republic from my power to the dominion of the senate and Roman people. And for this merit of mine, by decree of the senate, I was called Augustus and the doors of my temple were publicly clothed with laurel and a civic crown was fixed over my door and a gold shield placed in the Julian senate-house, and the inscription on that shield testified to the virtue, mercy, justice, and piety, for which the senate and the Roman people gave it to me. After that time, I exceeded all in influence (*auctoritate*), but I had no greater power (*potestatis*) than the others who were colleagues with me in each magistracy.[8]

The office of emperor so often seen as the eclipse of republican liberty was also its last remnant. In the reign of Augustus, the structures of the

---

odium populum Romanum regalis nominis tenuit, quantum tenuerat post obitum vel potius excessum Romuli desiderium." Marcus Tullius Cicero. *De Re Publica, De Legibus*, ed. Clinton Walker Keyes (Cambridge, MA: Harvard University Press, 2006), 162–63.

6 Monroe E. Deutsch, "I am Caesar not Rex," *Classical Philology*, vol. 23, no. 4 (Oct. 1928): 394–98.

7 Ronald Syme, *The Roman Revolution* (Oxford: Oxford University Press, 2002), 475.

8 Alison Cooley, *Res gestae divi Augusti: Text, Translation, and Commentary* (Cambridge: Cambridge University Press, 2009), 98.

Republic were initially supposed to be able to coincide with the monarchical authority of Caesar in virtue of this key distinction between coercive *potestas* and moral *auctoritas*. But within a few years the twin instruments of *Imperium proconsulare majus* and *tribunicia potestas* (universal executive power and the ability to initiate and veto legislation) were annexed to the person of the Augustus.

In his tenth letter St Leo the Great upholds the principle that "He who is to govern all, should be chosen by all."[9] St Augustine in the *De Libero Arbitrio* likewise takes it as obvious that this is the proper form of government for a virtuous nation.[10] The preference for republican[11] forms of government endured in the Church into the High Middle Ages despite the barbarian conquest of the Latin West and its government by hereditary kings. In 1054 Cardinal Humbert of Silva Candida—a pillar of the papally maximalist Gregorian reform movement—described the proper form of episcopal election: "According to the decrees of the holy fathers, anyone who is consecrated as a bishop is first to be elected by the clergy, then requested by the people and finally consecrated by the bishops of the province with the approval of the metropolitan. . . . Anyone who has been consecrated without conforming to all these three rules is not to be regarded as a true, undoubted, established bishop nor counted among the bishops canonically created and appointed."[12] In the thirteenth century St Thomas continued to advocate as an ideal the election of the rulers by the people. In the *Summa theologiae*, the best form of government is

---

9 St Leo the Great, Letter 10:6 (PL 54:634), in *Nicene and Post-Nicene Fathers*, Second Series [=*NPNF* II], vol. 12, ed. Charles Lett Feltoe (Buffalo, NY: Christian Literature Publishing Co., 1895), 11.

10 St Augustine of Hippo, *On the Free Choice of the Will*, trans. T. Williams (Hackett: Indianapolis, 1993), 10. See PL 32:1228–29.

11 In sense of Rome's popular *and* constitutionally mixed form observed from 509–27 BC.

12 Brian Tierney, *The Crisis of Church and State 1050–1300* (Toronto: University of Toronto Press, 1988), 40.

constructed from one supreme ruler and a group of co-rulers elected by the whole people from a free choice of all citizens.[13] The best method of legislation is the enacting of laws by the Senate and the People together.[14]

In its early centuries the empire was a patchwork of city-states: ancient polities in the Greek-speaking east and Latin new towns in the Celtic west beyond the Alps. These cities, however, had no share in the selection or exercise of imperial power. The popular acclamation of the emperor more often than not occurred on the battlefield, but the senate was fixed in Rome (until the creation of its twin in Constantinople in the fourth century). For papal elections, however, both elements were fixed in the capital. This fact was all the more significant as the capital had, since the third century, ceased to function as such except symbolically. Although it would take many, many centuries and several schisms for this fact to be vindicated in practice, the decrees of the Roman pontiffs were in theory as sweeping in their application as those of his temporal counterpart. As Valentinian III acknowledged in 445:

> Since, then, the primacy of the Apostolic See is established by the merit of St Peter (who is the chief among the bishops), by the majesty of the City of Rome, and finally by the authority of a holy council, no one, without inexcusable presumption, may attempt anything against the authority of that see. Peace will be secured among the churches if every one recognize his ruler. . . . Lest even a slight commotion should arise in the churches, or the religious order be disturbed, we herewith permanently decree that not only the bishops of Gaul, but those of the other provinces, shall attempt nothing counter to ancient custom without the authority of the venerable father [Papa]

[13] St Thomas Aquinas, *Summa theologiae* I-II, Q. 105, art. 1.

[14] St Thomas Aquinas, *Summa theologiae* I-II, Q. 95, art. 4. See also M. J. Wilks, *The Problem of Sovereignty in the Late Middle Ages* (Cambridge: Cambridge University Press, 1963), 203.

> of the Eternal City. Whatever shall be sanctioned by the authority of the Apostolic See shall be law to them, and to every one else; so that if one of the bishops be summoned to the judgment of the Roman bishop and shall neglect to appear, he shall be forced by the moderator of his province to present himself. In all respects let the privileges be maintained which our deified predecessors have conferred upon the Roman church.[15]

The Roman Church was far from oblivious to the parallel between its status and constitution and that of the empire. The practice of framing papal letters as if they were imperial rescripts goes back to the patristic age.[16] St Peter Damian in a letter (97) to the cardinal bishops in 1063 draws the spiritual lessons of their status as senators (at that time particularly prominent due to the popularity of the Pseudo-Isidorian Decretals):

> The Roman Church, moreover, which is the see of the apostles, should imitate the ancient assembly of the Romans. Just as formerly that earthly senate conducted all its discussions and directed and carefully exercised its common effort to subdue the whole non-Roman world to its authority, so now the custodians of the Apostolic See who are the spiritual senators of the universal Church, must earnestly engage in the exclusive effort to win the human race for the dominion of Christ, the true emperor. And as formerly the Roman consuls brought back trophies of victory from various parts of the world after defeating their enemies, so must these now free the captured souls of men from the land of the devil. They must always long for these honours of victory, those triumphs, so that they rejoice in snatching away the spoils of perishing souls from

15 James Harvey Robinson, *Readings in European History* (Ginn: Boston, 1905), 72.

16 D. L. d'Avray, *Papal Jurisprudence, 385–1234: Social Origins and Medieval Reception of Canon Law* (Cambridge University Press: Cambridge, 2022).

> the ancient robber and take them back as signs of victory to Christ, their king.[17]

In the *Duo Sunt* passage of his justly famous letter to the emperor Anastasius, Pope St Gelasius I, seeking to explain the distinction between the spiritual and temporal power, returns to Augustus's distinction between *potestas* and *auctoritas* and does something unexpected with it:

> There are two, august emperor, by which this world is chiefly ruled, namely, the sacred authority of the priests and the royal power. Of these, that of the priests is the more weighty, since they have to render an account for even the kings of men in the divine judgment. You are also aware, dear son, that while you are permitted honourably to rule over humankind, yet in things divine you bow your head humbly before the leaders of the clergy and await from their hands the means of your salvation. In the reception and proper disposition of the heavenly mysteries you recognize that you should be subordinate rather than superior to the religious order, and that in these matters you depend on their judgment rather than wish to force them to follow your will.[18]

In this way Gelasius takes the tension between authority and power upon which the foundational claim of the Roman emperors to have preserved liberty within the rule of law rests and maps it onto the distinction between the clerical and lay orders, restoring in a certain sense the insight which created the consulate a thousand years before.[19]

---

[17] Owen J. Blum, *The Letters of Peter Damian 91–120* (Washington, DC: Catholic University of America Press, 1998), 83.

[18] PL 59:42; DH 347.

[19] There is an interesting parallel in St Gregory the Great's "ministerial" understanding of the empire laid out in his letter to the emperor Maurice: "Ad hoc enim potestas super omnes homines dominorum meorum pietati cælitus data est, ut qui bona appetunt,

It is interesting to note that after the division of the empire into East and West two consuls were appointed in each half and that from the time Justinian absorbed the consulate into the imperial office the popes have (as have the Byzantine emperors) on at least two occasions sought to appoint Western consuls on their own authority. This fact seems to imply an absorbance of the Western consular office into the papacy. Thus, the limiting bifurcation of the executive power is replicated in the Gelasian distinction of temporal power and spiritual authority.

St Thomas's preference for the election of the "aristocracy" re-enters the more monarchical constitution of the Church through the institution of councils. For while each bishop is the monarch of his diocese he is also its representative in council, and while the pope may legislate and define for the whole church (for the chair must ultimately be free to determine whom he does and does not recognise as a member of the body over which he presides), the most fitting way for laws to be made and doctrinal questions to be finally settled is in council. As Bishop Gasser stated in his famous *Relatio*, "the most solemn judgment of the Church in matters of faith and morals is and always will be the judgment of an ecumenical council, in which the pope passes judgment together with the bishops of the Catholic world who meet and judge together with him."[20] And as *Lumen Gentium* (which cites Gasser three times in Chapter 3) puts it:

adjuventur; ut cælorum via largius pateat; ut terrestre regnum cælesti regno famuletur." PL 77:663.

20 James T. O'Connor, *The Gift of Infallibility: The Official Relatio on Infallibility of Bishop Vincent Ferrer Gasser at Vatican Council I* (San Francisco: Ignatius Press, 2008). This is surely because the promise of infallibility itself belonging to the pope alone and in council is purely negative while the promise of indefectibility is positive (the whole deposit of faith will never perish from the entire body of either episcopate or faithful) but attaches to the episcopate as a whole, not to the person of the pope. This is why the Council of Florence felt the need to justify the Holy See's unilateral adoption of the Filioque as arising "from imminent need." The implication is that the Holy See should not define unilaterally except from imminent need.

"The order of bishops, which succeeds to the college of apostles and gives this apostolic body continued existence, is also the subject of supreme and full power over the universal Church, provided we understand this body together with its head the Roman pontiff and never without this head."

There was a marked increase in the scale and intensity of social violence that became necessary to maintain orthodoxy in the Church after episcopal elections perished in practice, and then were forgotten as an ideal, from the thirteenth century onwards. This eventually became unsustainable in the early modern period. The First Vatican Council was very careful to define the limits of infallibility as regards both its object and its exercise, but this has not prevented subsequent generations of Catholics from treating every deliverance of the pontiff and even his prudential judgements as effectively infallible—with distinctly mixed results. The non-functioning "magisterium" of the dissident Eastern churches shows the impossibility of conciliar magisterium without an infallible chair. The collapse of belief and practice in the Latin West led by scandalously unfaithful "Catholic" politicians shows the catastrophic effect of a loss of that "eucharistic coherence" which is the precondition of a restored electoral episcopate. The eucharistic discipline that underpins the visibility of the Church as a social body united in faith and morals has been replaced by a Faustian bargain between clergy and laity: "you do not look into our faith and morals and we will not look into yours."

The Romanness of the Church and an appreciation of the same is essential both to the identity of the church and to her health. It is hoped that the following pages will make some contribution to this necessary process of self-rediscovery.

Introduction

> The inscription declaring the crime for which the Lord was condemned clearly showed that the crucified one was king and lord of practical, natural and theological philosophy, since the evangelist says that the inscription was written in Latin, Greek and Hebrew. I think that practical philosophy is denoted by the use of Latin, since according to Daniel, the kingdom of the Romans is stronger than any other in the world, and strength is the mark above all of practical philosophy. Natural learning I consider to be designated by the Greek language, since the Greeks studied natural philosophy more than other men. And theological teaching is denoted by the Hebrew, since this people from the beginning of its existence was clearly dedicated to God by reason of its ancestors.[21]

The idea that Greek philosophy was prepared by providence to aid the transmission of the gospel is a familiar one to faithful Catholics. The technical philosophical language afforded by Greek thought has played a key role in the formulation of the most exalted dogmatic definitions of the Church's greatest councils, safeguarding the mysteries of the Trinity, the Incarnation, and the Blessed Sacrament. As Paul VI teaches:

[21] Cyril of Alexandria, *Commentary on Luke*, PG 73:938.

> These formulas—like the others that the Church uses to propose the dogmas of faith—express concepts that are not tied to a certain specific form of human culture, or to a certain level of scientific progress, or to one or another theological school. Instead they set forth what the human mind grasps of reality through necessary and universal experience and what it expresses in apt and exact words, whether it be in ordinary or more refined language. For this reason, these formulas are adapted to all men of all times and all places.[22]

There is nothing arbitrary in this. The thought of the Greeks is not a convenient system that serves its purpose but might in principle have been exchanged for some other; rather it is the highest intellectual achievement of mankind, "a philosophical patrimony which is perennially valid."[23] In order for divine revelation to occur at all, especially in our world where the mystery and the destiny it reveals is so exalted that God could not even create a nature for which they would be proportionate and natural, it must be that those truths which are revealed be communicated by means of concepts which are themselves attainable by reason. If this were not so, not only the propositions but the words in which they were phrased would escape us and faith would be impossible. When revelation reached its completion, therefore, at the death of the last apostle,[24] it was necessary that the perennial philosophy be already in the world and accessible to the men of the apostolic age. This "horizon of universal, objective and transcendent truth"[25] is both universally applicable to all times and places and was attained and accomplished in a particular time and place in preparation for the Incarnation of the Eternal Word.

---

22 Paul VI, *Mysterium Fidei* (1965) §24.

23 Vatican II, *Optatam Totius* (1965) §15.

24 Pius X, *Lamentabili Sane* (1907) §21.

25 John Paul II, *Fides et Ratio* (1998) §44.

> While the world lasts, will Aristotle's doctrine on these matters last, for he is the oracle of nature and of truth. While we are men, we cannot help, to a great extent, being Aristotelians, for the great Master does but analyze the thoughts, feelings, views, and opinions of human kind. He has told us the meaning of our own words and ideas, before we were born. In many subject-matters, to think correctly, is to think like Aristotle; and we are his disciples whether we will or no, though we may not know it.[26]

And like all natural virtues this philosophical patrimony was taken up, perfected and not destroyed by grace,[27] and so scaled "heights unthinkable to human intelligence"[28] in the thought of St Thomas Aquinas. Thus,

> the capital theses in the philosophy of St. Thomas are not to be placed in the category of opinions capable of being debated one way or another, but are to be considered as the foundations upon which the whole science of natural and divine things is based; if such principles are once removed or in any way impaired, it must necessarily follow that students of the sacred sciences will ultimately fail to perceive so much as the meaning of the words in which the dogmas of divine revelation are proposed by the magistracy of the Church.[29]

Accordingly, these principles have been "unreservedly sanctioned" by the Church.[30]

But what of practical philosophy of which the Saviour is also king and lord and which is signified by the Latin language? What of the kingdom

[26] John Henry Newman, *The Idea of a University* (London: Longmans, Green, and Co., 1907), 109–10.

[27] Thomas Aquinas, *Summa theologiae* I, Q. 1, art. 8, ad 2.

[28] Leo XIII, Æterni *Patris* (1879) §4 and John Paul II, *Fides et Ratio* (1998) §44.

[29] Pius X, *Doctoris Angelici* (1914) §3.

[30] Pius XI, *Studiorum Ducem* (1923) §11.

of the Romans, stronger than any other in the world? Is this, too, "unreservedly sanctioned" by the Church? As it is fitting that the speculative preparation for the Incarnation should terminate in principles and in "a philosophical patrimony," so we might expect the practical preparation for the Incarnation to terminate in a concrete institution and its laws.

But if the Socratic philosophical tradition was tainted by pagan errors such that the labour of thirteen centuries and the greatest and saintliest minds that ever lived were needed to purify and perfect it, how many thousand times more must this be true of a blood-soaked empire, marching under heathen banners and built upon the backs of slaves? Happily, however, the greatest Father of the Church has already considered this question for us in the form of Augustine's *City of God*.

For Augustine, the zeal of men for conquest is the misdirected restlessness of those whom God made for Himself but who will not rest in Him: "the earthly city, which, though it be mistress of the nations, is itself ruled by its lust of rule." And yet, the strength of the Roman polity in putting down its enemies is only the manifestation of its internal constitution—of its "practical philosophy," to use St Cyril's expression—and the connection between them is not necessary:

> For, as far as this life of mortals is concerned, which is spent and ended in a few days, what does it matter under whose government a dying man lives, if they who govern do not force him to impiety and iniquity? Did the Romans at all harm those nations, on whom, when subjugated, they imposed their laws, except in as far as that was accomplished with great slaughter in war? Now, had it been done with the consent of the nations, it would have been done with greater success, but there would have been no glory of conquest, for neither did the Romans themselves live exempt from those laws which they imposed on others. Had this been done without Mars and Bellona, so that there should have been no place for victory,

> no one conquering where no one had fought, would not the condition of the Romans and of the other nations have been one and the same, especially if that had been done at once which afterwards was done most humanely and most acceptably, namely, the admission of all to the rights of Roman citizens who belonged to the Roman empire, and if that had been made the privilege of all which was formerly the privilege of a few? . . . For I do not see what it makes for the safety, good morals, and certainly not for the dignity, of men, that some have conquered and others have been conquered, except that it yields them that most insane pomp of human glory, in which they have received their reward.[31]

During the First World War Hilaire Belloc delivered a series of lectures which he later adapted into a book called *Europe and the Faith.* In the celebrated opening paragraph of chapter one he makes the following claim:

> The history of European civilization is the history of a certain political institution which united and expressed Europe, and was governed from Rome. This institution was informed at its very origin by the growing influence of a certain definite and organized religion: this religion it ultimately accepted and, finally, was merged in. The institution—having accepted the religion, having made of that religion its official expression, and having breathed that religion in through every part until it became the spirit of the whole—was slowly modified, spiritually illumined and physically degraded by age. But it did not die. It was revived by the religion which had become its new soul. It re-arose and still lives. This institution was first known among men as RES PUBLICA: we call it today "The Roman Empire." The Religion which informed and saved it was

[31] Augustine, *City of God*, V, 17, trans. M. Dods, *NPNF* I, vol. 2 (Buffalo, NY: Christian Literature Publishing Co., 1887), 98.

then called, still is called, and will always be called "The Catholic Church."[32]

The argument of this book is that Belloc is essentially right. The Church is a perfect society.[33] That is, it possesses within itself all the necessary means for the attainment of its end. Until God grants the grace to live the counsels in a state of perfection to all members of the Church (which perhaps He will do one day),[34] the ordering of temporal goods must form some part of the means necessary to the attainment of the Church's end. As this is precisely the responsibility of the temporal power,[35] the temporal order must therefore exist somehow *within* the Church. As Boniface VIII teaches, "in the Church and in her power are two swords."[36] Conversely, to attain its end the temporal community needs the favour of God, which

32 Hilaire Belloc, *Europe and the Faith* (London: Burns & Oates, 1962), 17. This passage famously concludes with the claim "Europe is the Church, and the Church is Europe." While certainly memorable, this claim has somewhat obscured the sense of Belloc's argument up to that point. Of course, by "Europe" he did not mean the Eurasian Atlantic Peninsula, he meant "Western Civilization" or "The West" in a cultural/social/political sense. But even then, Belloc's argument implies that the relationship between the Church and Western civilisation is analogous to that between soul and body, rather than being one of unnuanced identity.

33 Leo XIII, *Immortale Dei* (1885) §10.

34 Augustine, *On the Good of Marriage*, 10 (PL 40:380), trans. C.L. Cornish, in *NPNF* II, vol. 3 (Buffalo, NY: Christian Literature Publishing Co., 1895), 10. Cf. Richard Butler O.P., *Religious Vocation: An Unnecessary Mystery* (Chicago: H. Regnery Co., 1961), 94; Revelation 14:4.

35 Leo XIII, *Immortale Dei* §14. Leo XIII tellingly compares the proper relationship between the spiritual and the temporal powers to the orbits of heavenly bodies and to the union of soul and body. The former recalls the famous mediaeval simile of the sun and the moon, the latter (properly understood) implies that the spiritual power requires the temporal for its proper operation but not for its bare existence, while the temporal power when separated from the spiritual is, strictly speaking, no true commonwealth at all. This is precisely the doctrine of St Augustine in *The City of God*, which Leo XIII invokes at the beginning of the encyclical.

36 Boniface VIII, *Unam Sanctam* (1302), DH 870–75.

may be obtained only through the Church.[37] As an essential part of the identity of the Church militant, this lay power can never have been lacking to her. From the moment the Commonwealth of Israel was extinguished, therefore, some other sword must have been given to the Church. For "The kingdom of the world has become the kingdom of our Lord and of his Christ, and he shall reign for ever and ever."[38] In his tract on the Antichrist, St. John Henry Newman argues that the civil order of the modern West is an extension of the Roman state.[39] In his *Essay on the Development of Christian Doctrine*, one of the perennial features which Newman suggests will always be detected in the Church is that it is "a natural enemy to governments external to itself."[40] St Thomas Aquinas similarly holds that, rather than having perished, the Roman *imperium* survives until the end of time through the obedience shown to the Roman pontiff.[41] For Newman, insofar as the civil order established and licenced by the Romans persists in the world, the order of Christendom also persists and the final persecution of the Antichrist is delayed: "it is not clear that the Roman Empire is gone. Far from it: the Roman Empire in the view of prophecy, remains even to this day . . . the present framework of society and government, as far as it is the representative of Roman powers, is that which withholdeth, and Antichrist is that which will rise when this restraint fails." The project of this work is to argue, with Newman, Belloc, and Aquinas, that this lay power, the Iron Sceptre of the Son of Man, is the *Republica*—the Roman empire, the empire of Christian Rome—and that in her wayfaring state the Catholic Church is, consequently, necessarily Roman.

---

37 Leo XIII, *Libertas Praestantissimum* (1888) §14; *Diuturnum Illud* (1881).

38 Revelation 11:15.

39 St John Henry Newman, "The Patristical Idea of Antichrist," in *Discussions and Arguments* (London: Longmans, Green, and Co., 1907), 50–51.

40 St John Henry Newman, *An Essay on the Development of Christian Doctrine* (London: Longmans, Green, and Co., 1909), 208.

41 St Thomas Aquinas, *Super II Thess.*, cap. 2, lec. 1.

1

The Church Is Roman

On Saturday, May 7, 2005, Pope Benedict XVI took possession of the Lateran Basilica and of the Holy See. From that Chair the pontiff addressed the clergy and the people of Rome:

> Dear Romans, I am now your Bishop. Thank you for your generosity, thank you for your sympathy, thank you for your patience with me! As Catholics, in some way we are also all Romans. With the words of Psalm 87, a hymn of praise to Zion, mother of all the peoples, Israel sang and the Church sings: "Of Zion they shall say: 'One and all were born in her . . .'" (v. 5). We too can likewise say: as Catholics, in a certain way, we are all born in Rome.[42]

This is in many ways a remarkable statement, equating the City of Rome with the Zion of the New Covenant. And yet it is not a novelty but the ancient and enduring teaching of the Church rooted in Scripture, the Fathers, and the decrees of popes[43] and councils.

The first ecclesiastical writers to note the providential coincidence of the creation of the Augustan Principate and the Incarnation of the Eternal

42 Benedict XVI, *Homily for the Mass of Possession of the Chair of the Bishop of Rome*, May 7, 2005.

43 For example, he here echoes the famous claim of his predecessor and namesake Benedict XII that Rome, for Christians, is the universal *patria*. See Wilks, *Problem of Sovereignty*, 36.

Word were St Melito of Sardis[44] and Origen.[45] St Irenaeus of Lyons had already expressed approval for the peace brought to the world by the Romans under providence.[46] Tertullian, although in many ways no admirer of the Roman Imperium, eerily anticipated Constantine's Labarum by observing, in the sixteenth chapter of his Apology, the parallel between the Holy Cross and the standards of the Roman Legions.[47] Indeed, Tertullian's inadvertent anticipations of the absorption of the *Res Publica* by the Church are not infrequent.[48] Here at the end of the second century the North African is already using the Roman high-priestly title *Pontifex*

---

44 As quoted in Eusebius of Caesarea, *The History of the Church* (PG 5:1209 et seq.), trans. G.A. Williamson (London: Penguin, 1989), 134.

45 *Contra Celsum* 2:30.

46 Irenaeus of Lyon, *Adversus Haereses* 4.30.3: "Through their instrumentality the world is at peace, and we walk on the highways without fear, and sail where we will."

47 Tertullian, *Apologia*, 16. "Every stake fixed in an upright position is a portion of the cross; we render our adoration, if you will have it so, to a god entire and complete. We have shown before that your deities are derived from shapes modelled from the cross. But you also worship victories, for in your trophies the cross is the heart of the trophy. The camp religion of the Romans is all through a worship of the standards, a setting the standards above all gods. Well, all those images decking out the standards are ornaments of crosses. All those hangings of your standards and banners are robes of crosses. I praise your zeal: you would not consecrate crosses unclothed and unadorned." Trans. Sydney Thelwall, in *Ante-Nicene Fathers* [=*ANF*], vol. 3 (Buffalo, NY: Christian Literature Publishing Co., 1885), 31.

48 Tertullian, *De pallio*, 2 (PL 2:1087–90): "How large a portion of our orb has the present age reformed! How many cities has the triple power of our existing empire [see Johannes Quasten, *Patrology* (Notre Dame IN: Christian Classics, 2000), 2:316] either produced, or else augmented, or else restored! While God favours so many Augusti unitedly, how many populations have been transferred to other localities! How many peoples reduced! How many orders restored to their ancient splendour! How many barbarians baffled! In truth, our orb is the admirably cultivated estate of this empire; every aconite of hostility eradicated; and the cactus and bramble of clandestinely crafty familiarity wholly uptorn; and (the orb itself) delightsome beyond the orchard of Alcinoüs and the rosary of Midas. Praising, therefore, our orb in its mutations, why do you point the finger of scorn at a man?" See also *De pallio*, 1: "Blessings rain from the empire and from the sky."

Maximus of the bishop of Rome (albeit sarcastically)[49] and in a justly famous passage he remarks: "We are but of yesterday, yet we fill your cities, islands, forts, towns, councils, even camps, tribes, decuries, the palace, the senate, the forum; we have left you the temples alone."[50]

The climax of the Acts of the Apostles comes with the establishment by St Paul of his residence in Rome.[51] In his Epistle to the Romans, St Paul speaks of his longing to travel there[52] but also of his caution lest he build on another man's foundations:[53]

> From Jerusalem and as far round as Illyricum I have fully preached the gospel of Christ, thus making it my ambition to preach the gospel, not where Christ has already been named, lest I build on another man's foundation, but as it is written, "They shall see who have never been told of him, and they shall understand who have never heard of him." This is the reason why I have so often been hindered from coming to you. But now, since I no longer have any room for work in these regions, and since I have longed for many years to come to you, I hope to see you in passing as I go to Spain. . . .[54]

The citation made by St Paul here is Isaiah 52:15 (LXX) and the context is interesting. It is taken from the opening verses of the last song of the Suffering Servant:

> As many were astonished at him—his appearance was so marred, beyond human semblance, and his form beyond that of the sons of

49 Tertullian, *On Modesty*, 1 (PL 2:281). The pope is first called "pontiff" in an official text, fittingly enough, in the Edict of Thessalonica (380) which established the faith delivered by Peter to the Romans and preserved by "the Pontiff Damasus" as the criterion of orthodoxy.

50 Tertullian, *Apology*, 37 (PL 1:462–63).

51 Acts 28:16–31.

52 Romans 15:23.

53 Romans 15:22.

54 Romans 15:19–24.

> men—so shall he startle many nations; kings shall shut their mouths because of him; for that which has not been told them they shall see, and that which they have not heard they shall understand.[55]

The word used for kings here is βασιλευς—the same as that used in 1 Peter 2:17 and 1 Timothy 2:24 for the emperor (and much later on adopted as their official title).[56] The quotation from Isaiah thus serves to explain why St Paul delayed in coming to Rome and why he longed to come. God's vessel of election, to carry His name before the Gentiles and their kings,[57] naturally sought to appear before the emperor,[58] and yet he did not wish to infringe upon the jurisdiction of "another man." That other man must surely be St Peter who St Jerome tells us in *De Viris Illustribus*[59] occupied the "sacerdotal chair" at Rome for twenty-five years. St Peter disappears in the narrative of Acts at 12:17[60] when he is said, after his miraculous release from prison, without further elaboration, to have departed to another place. If, as seems logical given its ending prior to the martyrdom of either apostle, we take Acts to have been completed not much later than the beginning of the seventh decade of the first century, then Luke's discretion concerning the residence of the chief apostle in Rome is understandable. In 1 Peter 5:13 the apostle refers to his residence in "Babylon," which is generally taken to be the imperial capital (Babylon itself being a more or less abandoned ruin at this time)[61] but surely also indicates some reserve in explicitly revealing his location.

At the end of the first century St Clement asserted that the instructions he gave to the Corinthians were given through the inspiration

[55] Isaiah 52:14–15 (LXX).

[56] See below, p. 29.

[57] βασιλέων, Acts 9:15.

[58] Acts 22:25 and 25:21.

[59] St Jerome, *De Viris Illustribus*, 1 (PL 23:638).

[60] He appears again in chapter 15.

[61] Constantine refers to the ruined character of Babylon in his *Oration to the Assembly of the Saints*, ch. 16 (PL 8:445).

of the Holy Spirit.[62] St Ignatius of Antioch, a decade later, felt free to issue orders to the other churches on his route to the capital but not to the church of Rome, for he is neither Peter nor Paul.[63] St Irenaeus most famously declares towards the end of the second century that "all churches must agree with this church on account of its preeminent authority," that is, with that "very great, the very ancient, and universally known church founded and organized at Rome by the two most glorious apostles, Peter and Paul."[64] Pope Victor will later seek to impose the penalty of excommunication upon the church in Asia Minor for refusing to submit to the Roman date of Easter. St Victor was dissuaded from this drastic step by St Irenaeus himself, but not on the grounds that he lacked the authority.[65]

The case of Asia Minor and the Quartodeciman controversy is an interesting one. It shows that the church of Asia Minor, which would in 451 form the basis for the Patriarchate of Constantinople,[66] had a distinct liturgical tradition dating back to apostolic times and was already recognised as such in the second century. For all the questions that might be raised therefore about the very late claim of Constantinople to foundation by St Andrew,[67] it remains the case that the tradition of this jurisdiction is apostolic[68] (if not its association with Byzantium).[69]

62 St Clement of Rome, *Letter to the Corinthians*, in Andrew Louth, *Early Christian Writings: The Apostolic Fathers* (Harmondsworth, England: Penguin, 1987), 49.

63 St Ignatius of Antioch, *Letter to the Romans*, in Louth, *Early Christian Writings*.

64 St Irenaeus, *Adversus Haereses*, II.3.3 (PG 7:849).

65 Eusebius of Caesarea, *History of the Church*, 5:24 (PG 20:493–508).

66 Norman P. Tanner, *Decrees of the Ecumenical Councils*, vol. 1 (London: Sheed & Ward, 1990), 99–100. The term "patriarch" is, however, a later precision.

67 Francis Dvornik, *The Idea of Apostolicity in Byzantium and the Legend of the Apostle Andrew* (Washington, DC: Harvard University Press, 1958).

68 Adrian Fortescue, *The Orthodox Eastern Church* (London: Catholic Truth Society, 1908), 23–24.

69 See CCEO 57.

This issue of the patriarchates is significant because the Second Vatican Council "solemnly declares" in two places[70] that "the characteristic disciplinary autonomy, which the Eastern Churches enjoy . . . is not the result of privileges granted by the Church of Rome, but of the law itself which those Churches have possessed since apostolic times."[71] This would appear to be in contradiction to the teaching of Pope Eugenius IV in his Bull of Translation of the Council of Florence to the Lateran issued on October 14, 1443,[72] where he teaches that the Roman Church was founded by Christ alone[73] and itself founded all the other churches:

> For the Roman church founded all, whether the eminence of a patriarch or the seats of metropolitan primacy or of bishoprics or the dignities of churches of whatever rank; he alone, who entrusted to blessed Peter, the key-bearer of eternal life, the rights of the heavenly as well as of the earthly kingdom, founded the Roman church and straightaway set it on the rock of nascent faith.[74]

The only obvious way to reconcile these two teachings is to hold that the original autonomous jurisdictions of the East were all, like Rome, founded in the apostolic age with the approval of Peter himself.[75] This would mean that they were indeed founded by the head of the Roman Church but within the era of public revelation, allowing for their establishment to be an inspired act and preventing their overthrow. This would also explain

70 *Unitatis Redintegratio* §16 and *Orientalium Ecclesiarum* §5.

71 John Paul II's summary of the Conciliar teaching in *Euntes in Mundum* §1.

72 Tanner, *Decrees*, 1:583–86.

73 Also referred to as "The Holy Roman Church founded by the voice of Our Lord and Saviour" in *Cantate Domino* (Tanner, *Decrees* 1:570).

74 Quoting Nicholas II (Tanner, *Decrees*, 1:585). See also Pius XII, *Mystici Corporis Christi* (1943) §42, where he teaches that bishops receive their jurisdiction immediately from the Roman pontiff.

75 Cf. Galatians 2:9.

why the Council of Trent, in its thirteenth canon on the sacraments in general, solemnly defined the impossibility of overthrowing the received and approved Rites of the Church:

> If any one saith, that the received and approved rites of the Catholic Church, wont to be used in the solemn administration of the sacraments, may be contemned, or without sin be omitted at pleasure by the ministers, or be changed, by any pastor of the churches, into other new ones; let him be anathema.[76]

If the Church's Rites[77] are Patristic monuments ultimately traceable to the apostolic age, then they would quite naturally be immune to the vicissitudes of ecclesiastical positive law. As St Jerome observed, in such matters "each province may follow its own inclinations, and the traditions which have been handed down should be regarded as apostolic laws."[78] Even if each of the particular elements of each tradition cannot be traced with certainty or even plausibility to the apostles, the fact remains that as monuments to the Church's unwritten tradition[79] they cannot be abrogated by ecclesiastical authority, just as the authority of St Athanasius, St Augustine, or St John Chrysostom cannot be abrogated. The divinely instituted matter of many of the sacraments (olive oil, wine, bread) is taken from the staple crops of the Mediterranean world and the Rites which transmitted them objectively form part of the witness to the deposit of faith. The Church cannot repudiate them without repudiating herself and her Lord:

> This living transmission, accomplished in the Holy Spirit, is called Tradition, since it is distinct from Sacred Scripture, though closely

[76] DH 1613.

[77] A Rite is defined in CCEO 28.

[78] *NPNF* II, vol. 6, ed. W.H. Fremantle, G. Lewis and W.G. Martley (Buffalo, NY: Christian Literature Publishing Co., 1893).

[79] DH 1501.

> connected to it. Through Tradition, "the Church, in her doctrine, life and worship, perpetuates and transmits to every generation all that she herself is, all that she believes." "The sayings of the holy Fathers are a witness to the life-giving presence of this Tradition, showing how its riches are poured out in the practice and life of the Church, in her belief and her prayer."[80]

Vatican II likewise teaches that the Ritual Churches are the most fundamental unit of ecclesiastical organization after the universal and particular churches:

> The Holy Catholic Church, which is the Mystical Body of Christ, is made up of the faithful who are organically united in the Holy Spirit by the same faith, the same sacraments and the same government and who, combining together into various groups which are held together by a hierarchy, form separate Churches or Rites. Between these there exists an admirable bond of union, such that the variety within the Church in no way harms its unity; rather it manifests it, for it is the mind of the Catholic Church that each individual Church or Rite should retain its traditions whole and entire and likewise that it should adapt its way of life to the different needs of time and place.[81]

The idea that the ritual churches (of which there are seven)[82] are apostolic and original to the Church's structure is reinforced by the fact that representatives from the territory of each were present on the day of Pentecost itself.

---

[80] CCC 78.

[81] *Orientalium Ecclesiarum* §2.

[82] CCC 1203: "The liturgical traditions or rites presently in use in the Church are the Latin (principally the Roman rite, but also the rites of certain local churches, such as the Ambrosian rite, or those of certain religious orders) and the Byzantine, Alexandrian or Coptic, Syriac, Armenian, Maronite and Chaldean rites. In 'faithful obedience to

> When the day of Pentecost had come, they were all together in one place. And suddenly a sound came from heaven like the rush of a mighty wind, and it filled all the house where they were sitting. And there appeared to them tongues as of fire, distributed and resting on each one of them. And they were all filled with the Holy Spirit and began to speak in other tongues, as the Spirit gave them utterance. Now there were dwelling in Jerusalem Jews, devout men from every nation under heaven. And at this sound the multitude came together, and they were bewildered, because each one heard them speaking in his own language. And they were amazed and wondered, saying, "Are not all these who are speaking Galileans? And how is it that we hear, each of us in his own native language? Parthians and Medes and Elamites and residents of Mesopotamia, Judea and Cappadocia, Pontus and Asia, Phrygia and Pamphylia, Egypt and the parts of Libya belonging to Cyrene, and visitors from Rome, both Jews and proselytes, Cretans and Arabians, we hear them telling in our own tongues the mighty works of God."[83]

At the death of the last apostle, the seats of all these ritual churches lay within the frontiers of the Roman empire.

In fact, the most distant evidence of all confirms the point: the Nestorian Stele, the most ancient monument to the arrival of Christianity in China, set up in 781 by Chaldean Christians, is entitled "Memorial of the Propagation in China of the Luminous Religion from Rome."[84]

tradition, the sacred Council declares that Holy Mother Church holds all lawfully recognized rites to be of equal right and dignity, and that she wishes to preserve them in the future and to foster them in every way.'" See also CCEO 28, 58, and 59.

83 Acts 2:1–11.

84 It should be mentioned that, while the stele accounts for the Gospel in China going back to 635, according to Indian tradition the mission to China was initiated by the apostle Thomas in person shortly before his martyrdom (accounting for the site of his tomb on the eastern side of the subcontinent rather than near the Syro-Malabar

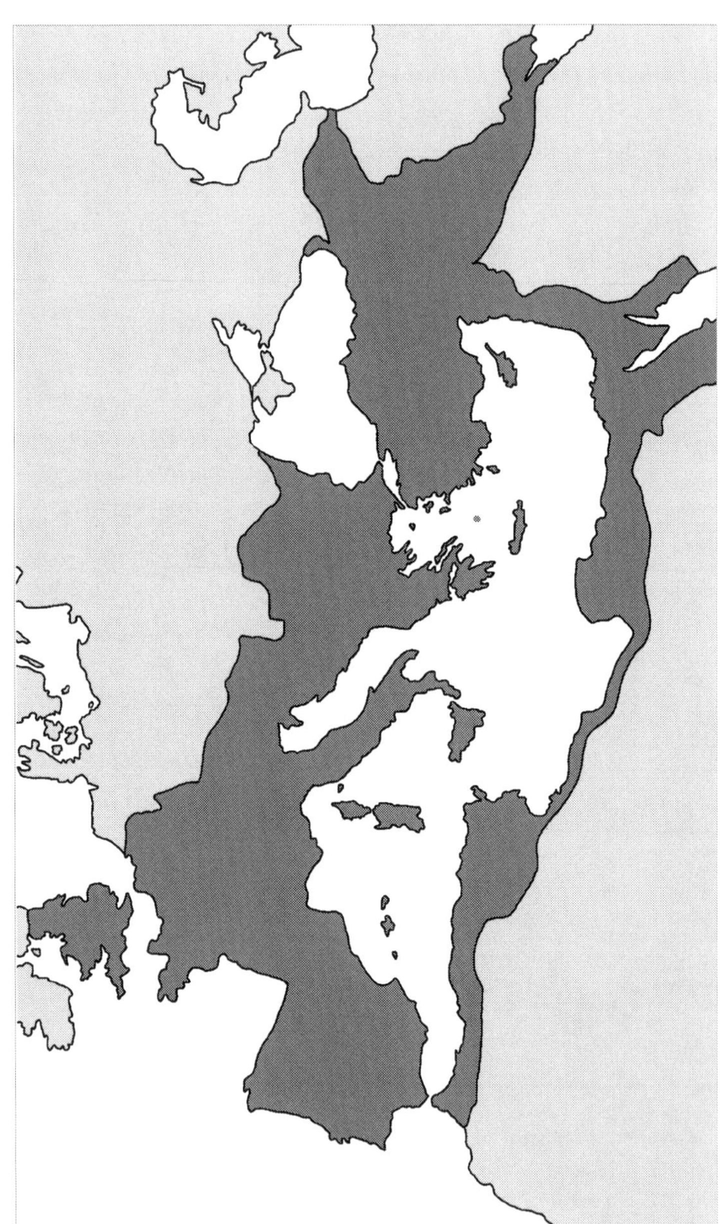

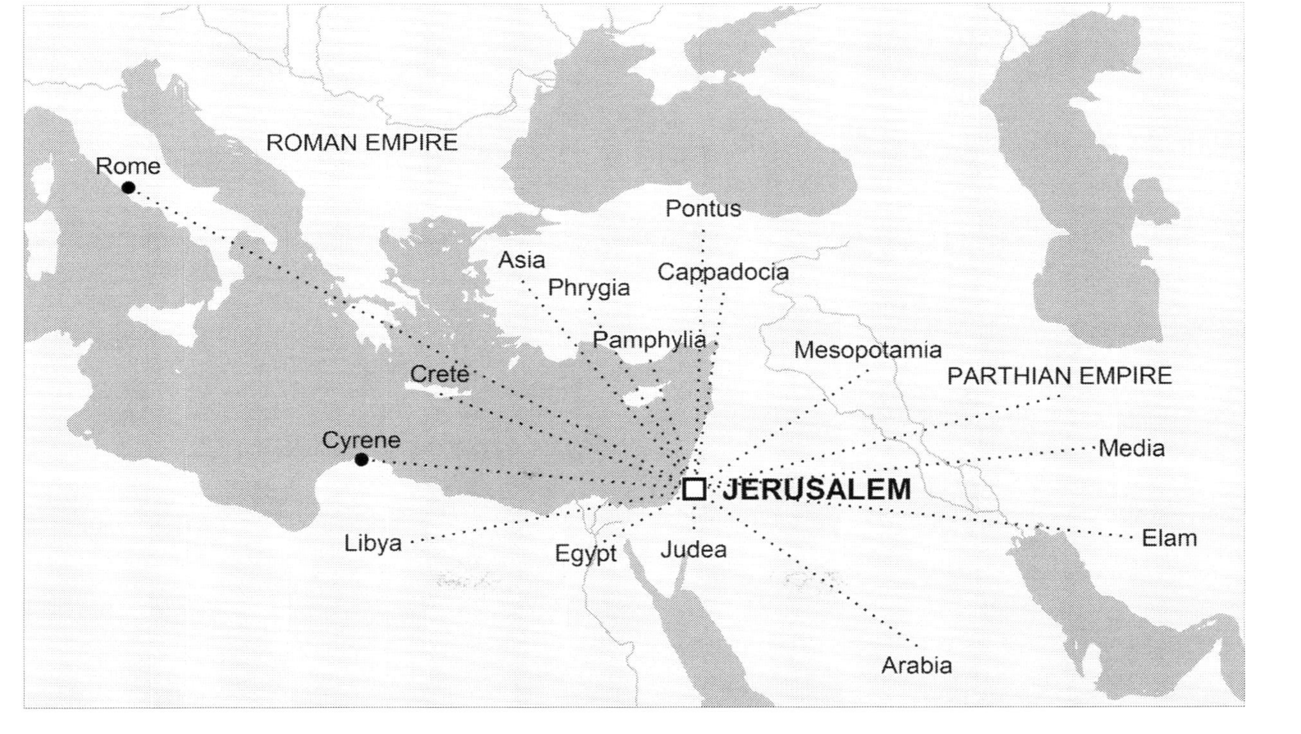
ROMAN EMPIRE
Rome
Pontus
Asia
Phrygia
Cappadocia
Pamphylia
Mesopotamia
PARTHIAN EMPIRE
Crete
Cyrene
Media
JERUSALEM
Libya
Egypt
Judea
Elam
Arabia

It is not of course merely as the context in which the liturgical tradition of each Rite developed that the Roman empire holds a privileged position, but also as the context in which almost all of the Fathers bequeathed their writings to the Church. For the few who lived amidst the conquerors of the empire (Patrick, Isidore, Bede, Damascene) rather than as its subjects, the importance of *Romanitas* was no less; in many ways it was greater.[85]

heartland). A.M. Mundadan, *History of Christianity in India: From the Beginning up to the Middle of the Sixteenth Century* (Bangalore: Church History Association of India, 1984), 1:30; cf. Bernard of St Thomas, *Mar–Thoma–Kristianikal*, 2 vols. (Mannanam, 1916/1921); enlarged one-volume reimpression by John Pellissery (Eranakulam: C.M.I. Publications/Kottayam: Pellissery Publications, 1992).

85 Despite the legions having departed from Britannia and himself living beyond the Irish Sea, St Patrick refers in his *Letter to the Soldiers of Coroticus* to "my fellow citizens, the holy Romans": Philip Freeman, *The World of St Patrick* (Oxford: Oxford University Press, 2014), 8. On Damascene, see Andrew Louth, *St. John Damascene: Tradition and Originality in Byzantine Theology* (Oxford: Oxford University Press, 2002), 204–5. In the *Ecclesiastical History of the English People* 1:1, St Bede points out that the different nations of Britain (English, British, Irish, and Picts) each "have their own language; but all are united in their study of God's truth by the fifth—Latin—which has become a common medium through the study of scriptures." St Bede, *Ecclesiastical History of the English People with Bede's Letter to Egbert and Cuthbert's Letter on the Death of Bede*, trans. Leo Sherley-Price (London: Penguin, 1990). St Bede also details with great approval the scrupulous *Romanitas* of St Benedict Biscop's foundation of his own monastery in Jarrow. The Vulgate of the Codex Amiatinus was produced with such exquisite attention to this point that, until the nineteenth century, it was widely held to have been produced in Rome itself! Michelle P. Brown, in *The Cambridge Companion to Bede*, ed. Scott DeGregorio (Cambridge: Cambridge University Press, 2010), 12. On the contrasting understandings of the Roman in Bede and Damascene, see the comments of Louth, *St John Damascene*, 283–84. Isidore of Seville, whose *Etymologies* provided a sort of encyclopaedia of *Romanitas* for the inhabitants of the Dark Ages, was described in the following terms by his contemporary Braulio of Saragossa: "After such misfortune in Spain in recent years, God encouraged him, as if he were setting up a prop—to preserve the ancient monuments, I believe, lest we decay into rusticity. To him we may fittingly apply the philosopher's comment [Cicero, *Academica Posteriora* 1.3]: 'Your books have brought us back, as if to our home, when we were roving and wandering in our own city like strangers, so that we might sometimes be able to

The cultural patrimony of the empire on a natural level is also crucial in the providential preparation for the Incarnation. Rome as an historical phenomenon is thus the bearer of natural and revealed wisdom given to us by God. As Pope John XXIII taught in his 1962 Apostolic Constitution *Veterum Sapientia*:

> The wisdom of the ancient world, enshrined in Greek and Roman literature, and the truly memorable teaching of ancient peoples, served, surely, to herald the dawn of the Gospel which God's Son, "the judge and teacher of grace and truth, the light and guide of the human race," proclaimed on earth. Such was the view of the Church Fathers and Doctors. In these outstanding literary monuments of antiquity, they recognized man's spiritual preparation for the supernatural riches which Jesus Christ communicated to mankind "to give history its fulfilment." Thus the inauguration of Christianity did not mean the obliteration of man's past achievements. Nothing was lost that was in any way true, just, noble and beautiful. The Church has ever held the literary evidences of this wisdom in the highest esteem. She values especially the Greek and Latin languages in which wisdom itself is cloaked, as it were, in a vesture of gold. She has likewise welcomed the use of other venerable languages, which flourished in the East. For these too have had no little influence on the progress of humanity and civilization. By their use in sacred liturgies and in versions of Holy Scripture, they

understand who and where we are. You have laid open the lifetime of our country, the description of the ages, the laws of sacred matters and of priests, learning both domestic and public, the names, kinds, functions and causes of settlements, regions, places and all matters both human and divine.'" *The Etymologies of Isidore of Seville*, trans. Stephen A. Barney (New York: Cambridge University Press, 2010), 8. When one examines the texts to which Braulio refers, it is clear that the homeland and city to which he alludes is the lost Imperium and not Spain. Indeed, the person to whom Cicero is referring is Varro, the great encyclopaedist of Pagan Rome.

> have remained in force in certain regions even to the present day, bearing constant witness to the living voice of antiquity. But amid this variety of languages a primary place must surely be given to that language which had its origins in Latium, and later proved so admirable a means for the spreading of Christianity throughout the West. And since in God's special Providence this language united so many nations together under the authority of the Roman empire—and that for so many centuries—it also became the rightful language of the Apostolic See.[86]

The Eastern Code[87] allows the translation of a Patriarchal See only for most grave reasons and with the consent of that Church's synod. Pope Pius IX in his 1864 *Syllabus of Errors* precludes the translation of the supreme pontificate. The thirty-fifth condemned proposition reads:

> There is nothing to prevent the decree of a general council, or the act of all peoples, from transferring the supreme pontificate from the bishop and city of Rome to another bishop and another city.[88]

If this might seem to leave open the possibility that the supreme pontiff himself might translate his office to another see,[89] this was excluded six years later by the Decrees of the First Vatican Ecumenical Council:

> For no one can be in doubt, indeed it was known in every age that the holy and most blessed Peter, prince and head of the apostles, the pillar of faith and the foundation of the Catholic Church, received

86 John XXIII, *Veterum Sapientia* (1962) §1 (AAS 54 [1962]: 129–30). Translation taken from *Adoremus Bulletin*, VIII.2 (April 2002).

87 CCEO 57.

88 DH 2935.

89 This interpretation would rely on reading "general council" loosely as merely the assembly and not properly as the entire college united to its head (see *Lumen Gentium* 22). For what a pope can do alone he most certainly can do with an ecumenical council.

> the keys of the kingdom from our Lord Jesus Christ, the saviour and redeemer of the human race, and that to this day and forever he lives and presides and exercises judgment in his successors the bishops of the Holy Roman See, which he founded and consecrated with his blood. Therefore, if anyone says that it is not according to the institution of Christ the Lord himself, that is, by divine law, that blessed Peter should have perpetual successors in the primacy over the whole Church; or if anyone says that the Roman Pontiff is not the successor of blessed Peter in the same primacy, let him be anathema.[90]

In the same document where he asserts the foundation of all jurisdictions by the Roman Church, Eugenius IV also says of Rome:

> In it our Saviour in his eternal providence settled the apostolic see in blessed Peter, prince of all the apostles, and on his right in fellowship the wondrous foresight of the same Saviour added the blessed apostle Paul. They are two bulwarks of the faith through whom the gospel shone in Rome; they are true fathers and true pastors; they are those who suffered on one day for merit, in one place for grace, under one persecutor for equal virtue, and made this city sacerdotal and royal and the capital of the world, as being the holy seat of Peter, and consecrated it to the Lord Christ with the glorious blood of martyrdom.[91]

---

[90] DH 3058.

[91] Tanner, *Decrees*, 1:585. In drafting the document that would become *Pastor Aeternus* (the First Dogmatic Constitution on the Church of Christ), the following canon was proposed: "If anyone says that it is not by the institution of Christ the Lord himself that blessed Peter should have perpetual successors in the primacy over the whole Church; or that the Roman pontiff is not by divine law the successor of blessed Peter in this primacy: let him be anathema." The conciliar minority was unhappy with this formulation. They did not consider that it was settled theologically that the fixity of

Vatican I in the Dogmatic Constitution *Dei Filius* applies the note Roman to the Church in addition to Holy, Catholic, and Apostolic.[92] In his 1943 Encyclical Letter *Mystici Corporis Christi*, Pius XII, citing Vatican I, repeats this identification even more explicitly:

> If we would define and describe this true Church of Jesus Christ—which is the One, Holy, Catholic, Apostolic and Roman Church—we shall find nothing more noble, more sublime, or more divine than the expression "the Mystical Body of Christ"—an expression which springs from and is, as it were, the fair flowering of the repeated teaching of the Sacred Scriptures and the Holy Fathers.[93]

---

the universal primacy at Rome is of divine law. There is, however, a certain ambiguity in the meaning of the expression "*de iure divino*." In the broad sense, it can be taken as referring to anything established as part of the deposit of faith and consequently irreversible, while in the narrow sense it can be taken as referring exclusively to things commanded by God in specific oral form such as the Law of Sinai or the *ipsissima verba* of Our Lord Jesus Christ in the Gospels. Innocent III had memorably asserted that the fixing of the supreme pontificate at Rome was divine law at least in the broader sense, in that it was an action of St Peter *ex revelatione divina*. The drafters of the constitution, playing on this proposal, reformulated the canon to read: "If anyone says that it is not by the institution of Christ the Lord himself (that is to say, by divine law) that blessed Peter should have perpetual successors in the primacy over the whole Church; or that the Roman pontiff is not the successor of blessed Peter in this primacy: let him be anathema." Members of the minority pointed out that this would still imply that the denial that a given Bishop of Rome was the universal primate would be heretical but their objections were ignored and the revised canon survived into the final draft adopted by the council and ratified by the pope, and thus the immovable fixity of the supreme pontificate at Rome entered into the extraordinary magisterium of the Church. See J. Michael Miller, *The Divine Right of the Papacy in Recent Ecumenical Theology* (Rome: Editrice Pontificia Università Gregoriana, 1980).

92 Norman P. Tanner, *Decrees of the Ecumenical Councils*, vol. 2 (London: Sheed & Ward, 1990), 803.

93 Pius XII, *Mystici Corporis Christi* §13.

Seven years later in the Encyclical *Humani Generis* he condemned those who did not feel bound by this doctrine:

> Some say they are not bound by the doctrine, explained in Our Encyclical Letter of a few years ago, and based on the sources of revelation, which teaches that the Mystical Body of Christ and the Roman Catholic Church are one and the same thing.[94]

The project of this work is to show the richness and authenticity of the Church's Roman character; the manner in which it integrates the Latin, Byzantine and other ritual traditions; and the implications of the church's *Romanitas* for the progress and resolution of salvation history. In what follows, the Scriptures are read canonically, with the Fathers and Doctors acknowledged as their privileged interpreters.

[94] Pius XII, *Humani Generis* (1950) §27.

2

Which Rome?

THE TERM "ROMAN CATHOLIC" can create a certain degree of misunderstanding. As we have seen, "Roman" was included as a note of the Church in the Creed of Pius IV issued at the end of the Council of Trent and solemnly reaffirmed by the fathers of Vatican I in the council's second session on January 6, 1870. Indeed, the celebrated decree of the Council of Florence *Cantate Domino*, adopted on February 4, 1442, defines many dogmas in the name of "the holy Roman church, founded on the words of our Lord and Saviour." Nevertheless, all these references could be taken as descriptions of the presiding local church of Rome acting as head of the episcopal college rather than of the Church as a whole. Indeed, the Creed of Pius IV explicitly refers to "the Holy, Catholic, Apostolic and Roman Church, *the mother and mistress* of all the Churches."

In the first Dogmatic Constitution of Vatican I, however—*Dei Filius*, "on the Catholic Faith," adopted on April 24, 1870—the adjective "Roman" is used in a context which seems more obviously intended to refer to the entire Church:

> The Holy, Catholic, Apostolic and Roman Church believes and acknowledges that there is one true and living God, creator and lord of heaven and earth, almighty, eternal, immeasurable, incomprehensible, infinite in will, understanding and every perfection.

In fact, an earlier version of this draft referred to the "Roman Catholic church"[95] and was objected to by the English bishops because it might be taken to validate the Anglican branch theory (see below). After some back and forth, the word "Roman" was placed at the end of the list to avoid this suggestion. This discussion implies the text was intended to refer to the Church as a whole.[96]

The sense in which the draft of *Dei Filius* had intended the expression and in which Pius XII used it was quite simply "the Mystical Body of Christ," that is, the Church without qualification. There are, however, three other senses in which the expression has been used and which give rise to confusion.

---

95 The first known official use of the precise phrase "Roman Catholic Church" dates to a papal letter of 1208 to some Armenian Christians. Michael M. Canaris, *Francis A. Sullivan, S.J. and Ecclesiological Hermeneutics* (Leiden: Brill, 2017), 116.

96 This ambiguity surrounding the meaning of the expression "Roman Church" would play a role in the formulation of the Irish Constitution in 1937. This text is rather overt in its Christian character, opening "In the Name of the Most Holy Trinity, from Whom is all authority and to Whom, as our final end, all actions both of men and States must be referred" and, in Article 44.1.1 acknowledging "that the homage of public worship is due to Almighty God." Nevertheless, the founders of the future Irish Republic wished both to tap into the long-offended Catholic sentiments of the majority of their countrymen and also to avoid the charge from Protestants (especially those of the severed six counties in the north) that the new Irish State was confessionally Catholic. Thus, in Article 44.1.2, they capitalised on the ambiguity contained in the Creed of Pius IV to give emphatic recognition to Catholicism without formally adopting it: "The State recognises the special position of the Holy Catholic Apostolic and Roman Church as the guardian of the Faith professed by the great majority of the citizens." The wording sounds resounding but, by omitting the word "one," it actually avoids formal recognition of Catholicism as the one true faith. Probably for this reason, the Papal Secretary of State Eugenio Cardinal Pacelli (the future Pius XII) refused formally to endorse the text. Hamish Fraser, the renowned Scottish former Communist leader and propagator of the Social Kingship of Christ, observed that the Irish Constitution of 1937 thus fell short of the just demands of the Saviour by one word—the very word "one."

The first and most appropriate of these three senses is the Arabic. In Middle Eastern usage, the "Roman Catholic" Church—*ar-Rūm al-Kāṯūlīk* (Arabic: روم الكاثوليك)—is the Ritual Church of those Catholics who observe the Rite of New Rome, i.e., Constantinople. In the West, these Catholics are generally known as Melkites, from the Syriac word *malkā* meaning "of the Basileus," the official title since AD 629 of the Roman emperor in Constantinople and his title in everyday Greek since the creation of the office (e.g., 1 Peter 2:17). The distinction arises from the Council of Chalcedon in 451. As the quarrel over the council's Christological definition crystallised, the adherents of the parallel Miaphysite hierarchy were preponderantly speakers of the Coptic and Syriac vernacular. The council was upheld by the government in Constantinople and adhered to largely by Greek speakers. Eventually, the Chalcedonians conformed to the liturgy of the capital as well. Thus Melkite became the name for Chalcedonian Christians using the liturgy of Constantinople in Egypt and Syria. After 1729 when Patriarch Cyril VI of Antioch restored communion with Pope Benedict XIII, the term Melkite or Roman Catholic became the name for those Chalcedonian Christians using the liturgy of Constantinople and in communion with the bishop of Rome. The celebrated orientalist and liturgical scholar Adrian Fortescue (who sought unsuccessfully to be transferred to the Melkite jurisdiction) observed that Melkite ought to be the term for all Catholics who observe the liturgy of Constantinople.[97]

The word "Byzantine" originally referred to the city of Byzantium prior to its refoundation as the second capital of the Roman empire by Constantine in 330. Thereafter it was used as a term for persons born in the city itself (not, however, in general for Roman citizens subject to the emperor in Constantinople). It was repurposed during the Crimean War by British and French historians to refer to the Roman empire governed

[97] Adrian Fortescue, *The Uniate Eastern Churches* (London: Burns & Oates, 1923), 8.

from Constantinople.[98] After the coronation of Charlemagne in 800, Latin westerners rapidly ceased to refer to Roman citizens subject to the emperor in Constantinople as "Romans" and began calling them instead "Greeks," their ruler emperor or king of the Greeks, and his dominions the empire or kingdom of the Greeks. If they were being diplomatic, they called it the empire of Constantinople or New Rome.[99] This refusal to concede the Romanness of the Roman empire governed from Constantinople was briefly interrupted between 1439 and 1453 when the Roman title of John VIII and Constantine XI was recognised due to the Union of Florence. Alas! the fall of the great city put paid to this happy interval and the more conventional Latin churlishness resumed and was indeed reinforced by the "Renaissance," because the championship of the line of emperors begun by Charlemagne was augmented and to some extent supplanted by a neo-classical snobbery which accepted the Roman credentials of neither the Constantinopolitan nor the Frankish rulers of the Middle Ages.

During the Crimean War the term "Empire of the Greeks" became a problem as it implied an historic claim over Constantinople for the new Greek nation state or the Orthodox world in general, neither of which suited the geopolitical interests of Britain and France. The much-abused Romans of the East were therefore rebaptised "Byzantines." This new nomenclature has since been adopted for liturgical and ecclesiastical purposes to describe Chalcedonian Christians of the Constantinopolitan Rite, with the variation "Byzantine Catholic" for those in communion with Rome.

In the English-speaking world, the term "Roman Catholic" was invented by Protestant Elizabethans when they were trying not to be too aggressive in their references to the Faithful but were nevertheless unwilling to concede the unqualified use of the term Catholic to them. Accordingly, Catholics

---

98 See Anthony Kaldelis, *Byzantium Unbound* (Leeds: Arc Humanities Press, 2019).

99 Paolo Squatriti, *The Complete Works of Liudprand of Cremona* (Washington, DC: Catholic University of America Press, 2007), 268.

refused to use it of themselves. It seems the approach of the Faithful softened a little when the prospect of emancipation was dangled in front of them, but then hardened again in the Second Spring.[100] The difficulty came with the insistence of officialdom upon the use of the "Roman Catholic" expression.[101]

The 1912 *Catholic Encyclopaedia* defines the term rather well: "A qualification of the name Catholic commonly used in English-speaking countries by those unwilling to recognize the claims of the One True Church."[102] It notes that in 1901 the English Hierarchy found they would not be permitted to address Edward VII on his accession unless they accepted the label. Cardinal Vaughan finally agreed so long as it was understood that he would clarify its meaning in a later public statement. He made this statement in a speech given at Newcastle upon Tyne[103] that September, where he told the faithful:

> I would now say to you all, use the term "Roman Catholic." Claim it: defend it: be proud of it; but in the true and Catholic sense. As the African Fathers wrote some fourteen centuries ago, "To be Roman is to be Catholic, and to be Catholic is to be Roman." But I would also say, like your English forefathers and your brethren on the Continent, call yourselves habitually and especially when the word "Roman" is misunderstood simply Catholics, members of the Catholic Church.[104]

---

[100] That is, the period of about a century from the restoration of the hierarchy to the end of the nineteen-fifties in which the Catholic Church experienced tremendous growth and cultural flourishing in England.

[101] Herbert Thurston, "Roman Catholic," in *The Catholic Encyclopedia* (New York: Robert Appleton Company, 1912).

[102] Ibid.

[103] A highly appropriate location. See Pius II, *Commentaries*, vol. 1 (London: Harvard University Press, 2003), 26.

[104] J. G. Snead-Cox, *The Life of Cardinal Vaughan*, vol. 2 (London: Herbert and Daniel, 1910), 238.

The problem is the use of the term "Roman" as a specific difference, as if there were other Catholics than those in communion with Rome. This problem is magnified outside (and now to an extent inside) the English-speaking world by the Empress Maria Theresa's invention of the term "Greek Catholic" to describe Catholics of the Byzantine Rite.[105] This causes enormous confusion. The term is inoffensive in itself although the increasingly popular "Byzantine Catholic" is perhaps better (resolving the difficulty of the "Greek" Catholic Church and of "Greek Catholics" who are not Greek Catholics). The problem is the tendency it creates of using the term "Roman Catholics" to describe Catholics of the Roman Rite, thereby reintroducing the idea that "Roman" names a sub-group and is not a universal property of all Catholics.[106]

The absurdity is put into relief by the fact that the pre-1453 (or pre-1261)[107] Byzantines themselves, as well as later Balkan Greek speakers down to the First World War and Byzantine Christians in the Middle East today, all insisted (and insist) that they were/are Romans and in the earlier period scorned the term "Greek" as equivalent to "Pagan."[108] This spurious historical mirage, "the Byzantine empire," has obscured the Roman identity of the Church, while the truth about the empire of New Rome is that its self-understanding and that of its people only strengthens the Romanness of the Church. The "Byzantine empire" *never existed*. It is an idea that no one would have recognised at the time, invented by hostile

105 John-Paul Himka, *Religion and Nationality in Western Ukraine: The Greek Catholic Church and the Ruthenian National Movement in Galicia, 1870–1900* (Montreal: McGill-Queen's University Press, 1999), 5.

106 Adrian Fortescue, *The Uniate Eastern Churches* (Piscataway, NJ: Gorgias Press, 2001), 1–3; 27.

107 Cf. Joseph Gill, *Byzantium and the Papacy, 1198–1400* (New Brunswick, NJ: Rutgers University Press, 1979).

108 Alexander P. Kazhdan, "Hellenes," in *The Oxford Dictionary of Byzantium*, vol. 2 (Oxford: Oxford University Press, 1991).

(or at least contemptuous) Western historians long after the Empire in Constantinople came to an end in 1453.[109] The Byzantine empire *is* the Roman empire. That is what its people called it; that is what it was.[110]

Thus the term "Roman Catholic" should not be used to describe Catholics of the Roman Rite as distinct from Catholics of the other Rites. A Catholic of the Roman Rite is a Roman-Rite Catholic or a Latin Catholic. There is no such thing really as the "Latin Rite" (unless you mean the Gallican Rite), since the Roman Rite was not originally in Latin nor, even when it was, was it exclusively so.[111] The term "Greek Catholic" is also not an especially helpful term,[112] though not a serious problem as long as it is not contradistinguished from "Roman Catholic"; the term "Byzantine Catholic" is better. The term "Roman Catholic" should only ever be used in Cardinal Vaughan's sense of Catholic *simpliciter*: to be Roman is to be Catholic, and to be Catholic is to be Roman.

---

[109] Cyril Mango, *The Oxford History of Byzantium* (Oxford: Oxford University Press, 2002), 1–2.

[110] Anthony Kaldellis, *Romanland: Ethnicity and Empire in Byzantium* (Cambridge MA: Harvard University Press, 2019).

[111] Adrian Fortescue, *The Mass: A Study of the Roman Liturgy* (Fitzwilliam, NH: Loreto Publications, 2005), 38.

[112] Although one might claim for it the authority of the Council of Florence in that "Greeks" and "Latins" are the terms used in *Laetentur Caeli* (1439) to denote the two parties to the misunderstandings it sought to resolve. DH 1301.

3

Why the Church Is Roman: Prophecy

IN THE CELEBRATED ENTRY in the Roman Martyrology for Christmas Day, traditionally read out before Midnight Mass, great emphasis is placed upon the convergence of Hebrew, Greek, and Roman reckonings for the measurement of years at the moment of the Incarnation. The passage ends:

> . . . in the sixty-fifth week according to the prophecy of Daniel; in the one hundred and ninety-fourth Olympiad; the seven hundred and fifty-second year from the foundation of the city of Rome; the forty-second year of the reign of Octavian Augustus; the whole world being at peace, in the sixth age of the world, Jesus Christ the eternal God and Son of the eternal Father, desiring to sanctify the world by his most merciful coming, being conceived by the Holy Spirit, and nine months having passed since his conception, was born in Bethlehem of Judea of the Virgin Mary, being made flesh. The Nativity of our Lord Jesus Christ according to the flesh.[113]

The passage situates the Incarnation in the context of the dating systems of the three cultures whose languages were affixed to the Cross: the Jews, the Greeks, and the Romans.[114] A prominent place is given to Octavian

113 Raphael Collins and Joseph B. Collins, *The Roman Martyrology* (Fitzwilliam, NH: Loreto, 2000), 290.

114 St Isidore, *Etymologies*, 191.

Augustus, the first Roman emperor, and his claim to have introduced universal peace. It was this claim which allowed him for the first time in many centuries to take the dramatic symbolic step of closing the gates of the Temple of Janus in Rome, indicating that the Roman Republic was at peace on and within all of its frontiers. In Augustus's own view, this meant *ipso facto* that the whole world was at peace, for, as the preface to his *Res Gestae* serenely begins, "these are the acts of the Deified Augustus by which he placed the whole world under the sovereignty of the Roman people."[115] Augustus goes on to record the achievement of universal peace under his principate:

> Our ancestors wanted Janus Quirinus to be closed when peace had been achieved by victories on land and sea throughout the whole empire of the Roman people; whereas, before I was born, it is recorded as having been closed twice in all from the foundation of the city, the senate decreed it should be closed thrice when I was leader (*princeps*).[116]

The limitless nature of the Roman dominion in time and space was famously promised by Jupiter to Venus (the mother of Aeneas) in the first book of Virgil's *Aeneid*: "For these I set no bounds in space or time; but have given empire without end."[117] Virgil was also responsible for the even more emphatic and extravagant promise of a new golden age described in

---

[115] "Rerum gestarum divi Augusti, quibus orbem terrarum imperio populi Romani subiecit." Cooley, *Res gestae divi Augusti*, 72.

[116] "Ianum Quirinum, quem claussum esse maiores nostri voluerunt, cum per totum imperium populi Romani terra marique esset parta victoriis pax, cum prius, quam nascerer, a condita urbe bis omnino clausum fuisse prodátur memoriae, ter me principe senatus claudendum esse censuit."

[117] *Aeneid* 278–79: "His ego nec metas rerum nec tempora pono; imperium sine fine dedi." *Virgil: Eclogues. Georgics. Aeneid: Books 1–6*, trans. H. R. Fairclough (Cambridge MA: Harvard University Press, 1999), 280–81.

the Fourth Eclogue: when the primeval bliss shall be restored by a newborn son of Jove, "flocks afield Shall of the monstrous lion have no fear. Thy very cradle shall pour forth for thee Caressing flowers. The serpent too shall die."[118] But Augustus had no sons and only one daughter, and his grandsons by her all died without succeeding to his newly minted office. The dynasty which (for all that) reigned after him was defaced by madness, tyranny, and debauchery, and by the death of Nero in AD 68 was extinct. The chaos that followed the extinction of the Julio-Claudian line coincided with the First Jewish Revolt and the destruction of the Temple. From both these wars arose Titus Flavius Vespasianus to found a new dynasty.[119] The fact that Vespasian came to the Purple from a war in Judea was not missed at the time. Whether or not anyone before Constantine[120] noticed the parallels between the prophesies of Virgil and Isaiah, there was much speculation surrounding a prophecy that the holder of universal empire would emerge from Judea.

Suetonius records:

> There had spread over all the Orient an old and established belief, that it was fated at that time for men coming from Judaea to rule the World. This prediction, referring to the Emperor of Rome, as afterwards appeared from the event, the people of Judaea took to themselves.[121]

Tacitus, also writing in the age of the Antonines, concurs, telling us the source of this belief in general terms:

---

[118] *Eclogue* IV 21–24: "nec magnos metuent armenta leones; ipsa tibi blandos fundent cunabula flores, occidet et serpens." Fairclough, *Virgil*, 50–51.

[119] With which St Clement I has occasionally been associated by blood or (less ambitiously but more plausibly) as a freedman. L. Cassius Dio, *Roman History* 67, 14.

[120] *Oration of Constantine to the Assembly of the Saints*, 20 (PL 8:453–66).

[121] Suetonius, *Lives of the Caesars*, trans. J.C. Rolfe (Harvard, MA: Loeb, 1997), 273: "Vespasian," 4.

> In most there was a firm persuasion, that in the ancient records of their priests was contained a prediction of how at this very time the East was to grow powerful, and rulers, coming from Judaea, were to acquire universal empire. These mysterious prophecies had pointed to Vespasian and Titus, but the common people, with the usual blindness of ambition, had interpreted these mighty destinies of themselves, and could not be brought even by disasters to believe the truth.[122]

The great Jewish historian Flavius Josephus (who, as the name suggests, had rather close links by this time with the new dynasty) agrees as to the origin of the prophesy and its true meaning:

> But now, what did most elevate them in undertaking this war was an ambiguous oracle that was also found in their sacred writings, how, "at that time, one from their country should become governor of the habitable earth." The Jews took this prediction to belong to themselves in particular; and many of the wise men were thereby deceived in their determination. Now, this oracle certainly denoted the government of Vespasian who was appointed emperor in Judea.[123]

Yet the line of Vespasian would also end in one generation, nor would Vespasian, though a competent emperor, obviously outshine the great Augustus. What none observed was that another dynasty of universal rulers situated at Rome but arising from Judea had also been established at precisely the same time. A year before Nero's death St Peter was handed over for execution and St Linus was the first to succeed to the Supreme Pontificate.[124]

---

[122] Tacitus, *The Complete Works of Tacitus*, trans. Alfred John William Church, et al. (New York: Modern Library, 1942), 665.

[123] Josephus, *War* 6.5.4, in *Josephus: The Complete Works*, trans. William Whiston (Nashville, TN: Thomas Nelson Publishers, 2003), 891.

[124] *The Book of the Popes (Liber Pontificalis)*, trans. L.R. Loomis (New York: Columbia University Press, 1916), 6.

What then was the prophecy that excited the Jews and the Romans of a universal dominion arising in Judea at the height of the Roman empire? The Roman Martyrology has already afforded the answer: "In the sixty-fifth week according to the prophecy of Daniel." This is an allusion to the prophecy contained in the ninth chapter of the Book of the Prophet Daniel. This text is justly famous as the single most explicit prophecy of Christ in the entire Old Testament.[125]

The Prophecy is striking from a number of perspectives. It occurred in the first year of the reign of Darius the Mede, an impossibly obscure figure the controversy about whose identity cannot be examined here.[126] Suffice it to say that he either is Cyrus the Great of Persia, or reigned concurrently with him or later than him. The Prophet Jeremiah had foretold that Judah would "serve" Babylon for seventy years.[127] There is some confusion about this prophecy, whether it refers to the period during which Judah was in the power of Babylon, in which case it is probably fair to say it corresponds to the period 609/8—539/38 BC, which is exactly seventy years. If it corresponded to the period of Daniel's own captivity, then it had two or three years left to run. If it corresponded to the period from the fall of Jerusalem, then it had a full twenty-two years left to run. The chapter therefore begins with Daniel seeking enlightenment from God concerning the meaning of the prophecy. He rehearses the sins of the people, which have brought upon them the curses contained in the Law of Moses, and begs for forgiveness. At length the angel Gabriel appears to Daniel to enlighten him.

Gabriel's answer is very strange. As we have seen, it would appear that the seventy years are about to be fulfilled and Judah is about to be returned

---

125 St Athanasius, *De Incarnatione*, 39. See Roy H. Schoeman, *Salvation Is from the Jews* (San Francisco: Ignatius Press, 2003), 81–82.

126 Louis F. Hartman and Alexander A. Di Lella O.F.M., *The Book of Daniel* (New York: Doubleday, 2005).

127 Jeremiah 25:9–12; Jeremiah 29:10; 2 Chronicles 36:20–23.

to Jerusalem. Not according to Gabriel. In fact the seventy years refer to a period of seventy times seven years and have not even begun yet:

> Seventy weeks are decreed upon thy people, and upon thy holy city, that transgression may be finished, and sin may have an end, and iniquity may be abolished; and everlasting justice may be brought; and vision and prophets may be fulfilled; and the saint of saints may be anointed. Know thou therefore, and take notice: that from the going forth of the word, to build up Jerusalem again, unto Christ the prince, there shall be seven weeks, and sixty-two weeks: and the street shall be built again, and the walls in straitness of times. And after sixty-two weeks Christ shall be slain: and shall have nothing; and the people of the prince who is to come shall destroy the city and the sanctuary: and the end thereof shall be waste, and unto the end of the war the appointed desolation. And he shall confirm the covenant with many, in one week: and in the half of the week the victim and the sacrifice shall fall: and there shall be in the temple the abomination of desolation: and the desolation shall continue even to the consummation, and to the end.[128]

Quite apart from the content (which is obviously highly significant) the precision of the dating of this prophecy is staggering. This is because "the going forth of the word, to build up Jerusalem again" may be precisely dated to the year 458/57 BC when the Persian Great King Artaxerxes empowered Ezra to rebuild the city of Jerusalem at public expense.[129] This rebuilding took "seven weeks," i.e., forty-nine years. Another "sixty-two weeks" (four hundred and thirty-four years) later brings one to the year AD 26 and the appearance and the anointing of Christ the Prince, i.e., the Baptism in the Jordan. After "half a week" (three and a half years), in

[128] Douay-Rheims (Challoner), partially revised to conform to the New Vulgate.

[129] Ezra 7:11–26.

AD 30 Christ the prince is slain, bringing to an end "the victim and the sacrifice" (as even the Talmud attests).[130] Another "half a week" later, in AD 33 St Paul, God's chosen vessel to bear His name among the Gentiles and their kings,[131] is converted, and Cornelius the first Gentile is baptised, and so the "covenant with many" is confirmed.[132] This last fact is rather significant, as is the fact that St Paul himself is a Roman citizen. For the present purposes, the most startling statement is that which follows in verse twenty-six, "and the people of the prince who is to come shall destroy the city and the sanctuary." No doubt the ability of the Judeans of the first century to make such precise calculations was limited, but as *inter alia* Tacitus, Suetonius, and Josephus bear witness, messianic speculation was frenetic and this last verse would seem to confirm that the people who would destroy the Temple and the city would be the Messiah's own people. What could be more natural then than Josephus's conclusion that Vespasian was the Messiah? Natural but wrong, and hardly compatible with the idea of the Messiah being "cut off" (Daniel 9:26). In fact, the implications are more startling still: that the people of the Prince who is to come, of the Messiah who was cut off in AD 30, who brought an end to victim and sacrifice and confirmed the covenant with the many, are the Romans.

The first explicit references to Rome in Scripture are contained in the Books of the Maccabees. The references are positive. Rome is a mighty ally of the Hasmonean revolution. Its military prowess and republican political system are described with admiration by the sacred author.[133] The fullest treatment is in the first book of the Maccabees, chapter eight:

---

[130] Rosh Hashanah 31b. See Schoeman, *Salvation is from the Jews*, 83.

[131] Acts 9:15.

[132] Acts 8–10. Paul Barnett, *Jesus and the Rise of Early Christianity: A History of New Testament Times* (Downers Grove, IL: InterVarsity Press, 1999), 21.

[133] The identity of the author of 1 Maccabees is unknown although he appears to be different from the author of 2 Maccabees. J. C. Dancy, *A Commentary on I Maccabees* (Oxford: Basil Blackwell, 1954).

Now Judas heard of the fame of the Romans, that they were very strong and were well-disposed toward all who made an alliance with them, that they pledged friendship to those who came to them, and that they were very strong. Men told him of their wars and of the brave deeds which they were doing among the Gauls, how they had defeated them and forced them to pay tribute, and what they had done in the land of Spain to get control of the silver and gold mines there, and how they had gained control of the whole region by their planning and patience, even though the place was far distant from them. They also subdued the kings who came against them from the ends of the earth, until they crushed them and inflicted great disaster upon them; the rest paid them tribute every year. Philip, and Perseus king of the Macedonians, and the others who rose up against them, they crushed in battle and conquered. They also defeated Antiochus the Great, king of Asia, who went to fight against them with a hundred and twenty elephants and with cavalry and chariots and a very large army. He was crushed by them; they took him alive and decreed that he and those who should reign after him should pay a heavy tribute and give hostages and surrender some of their best provinces, the country of India and Media and Lydia. These they took from him and gave to Eumenes the king. The Greeks planned to come and destroy them, but this became known to them, and they sent a general against the Greeks and attacked them. Many of them were wounded and fell, and the Romans took captive their wives and children; they plundered them, conquered the land, tore down their strongholds, and enslaved them to this day. The remaining kingdoms and islands, as many as ever opposed them, they destroyed and enslaved; but with their friends and those who rely on them they have kept friendship. They have subdued kings far and near, and as many as have heard of their fame have feared them. Those whom they wish to help and to make kings, they make kings, and those whom they wish they depose; and they have been greatly exalted. Yet for all this not one of them has put on a crown or worn purple as a mark of pride, but they have built for themselves a senate chamber, and every day three hundred and twenty senators constantly deliberate concerning the people, to govern them well. They trust one man each year to rule over them and to control all their land; they all heed the one man, and there is no envy or jealousy among them.

So Judas chose Eupolemus the son of John, son of Accos, and Jason the son of Eleazar, and sent them to Rome to establish friendship and alliance, and to free themselves from the yoke; for they saw that the kingdom of the Greeks was completely enslaving Israel. They went to Rome, a very long journey; and they entered the senate chamber and spoke as follows: "Judas, who is also called Maccabeus, and his brothers and the people of the Jews have sent us to you to establish alliance and peace with you, that we may be enrolled as your allies and friends." The proposal pleased them, and this is a copy of the letter which they wrote in reply, on bronze tablets, and sent to Jerusalem to remain with them there as a memorial of peace and alliance: "May all go well with the Romans and with the nation of the Jews at sea and on land for ever, and may sword and enemy be far from them. If war comes first to Rome or to any of their allies in all their dominion, the nation of the Jews shall act as their allies wholeheartedly, as the occasion may indicate to them. And to the enemy who makes war they shall not give or supply grain, arms, money, or ships, as Rome has decided; and they shall keep their obligations without receiving any return. In the same way, if war comes first to the nation of the Jews, the Romans shall willingly act as their allies, as the occasion may indicate to them. And to the enemy allies shall be given no grain, arms, money, or ships, as Rome has decided; and they shall keep these obligations and do so without deceit. Thus on these terms the Romans make a treaty with the Jewish people. . . ."[134]

Much of this passage is reported speech. It outlines the basis upon which Judas Maccabaeus decided to enter an alliance with the Romans. Consequently, although it may be accused of certain inaccuracies concerning Roman public law and military/diplomatic history, this is not a problem for inerrancy.[135] The enthusiasm for the Roman political system is interesting, however, given the civic (rather than ethnic) character of Roman patriotism and the role this "practical philosophy" would come to play in the new covenant. As it happens, the Roman Senate did not meet every day and the statement "They trust one man each year to rule over them and to control all their land; they all heed the one man, and there is no envy or jealousy among them" can only be said to describe the Consular office at a considerable stretch[136] (although Challoner has a go).[137] There are various arguments for supposing the text about India, etc., to be corrupt.[138] The embassy itself is attested by contemporary secular evidence.[139] For the task in hand what matters are the considerations Judas thought important in justification of an alliance with a pagan power. Resistance to the *de facto* ruler required some justification given prophetic opposition in the past to such action.[140] It was one thing, compelled by necessity, violently to resist

134 1 Maccabees 8:1–29.

135 Thomas Corbishley S.J., "1 and 2 Maccabees," in *A Catholic Commentary on Holy Scripture*, ed. B. Orchard, et al. (London: Nelson, 1953), 713.

136 Andrew Lintott, *The Constitution of the Roman Republic* (Oxford: Oxford University Press, 1999).

137 *The Holy Bible*, rev. Richard Challoner (London: Baronius Press, 2003).

138 Corbishley, "1 and 2 Maccabees," 713; Jonathan A. Goldstein, *I Maccabees* (New York: Doubleday, 1976), 352.

139 Goldstein, *I Maccabees*, 346.

140 II Chronicles 36:13–19 and Ezekiel 17:11–21 imply that God is offended by the violation of pledged loyalty to the Babylonian suzerain. Jeremiah 27:1–15 on the other hand

the specific command to violate God's law, but to form an alliance with a foreign power implied sovereignty: full emancipation from the rule of the Seleucids. The chapter is accordingly of great importance indicating that the resistance forced upon the Hasmoneans has effectively led to the forfeiture by Demetrius I of the status of *de facto* ruler.[141]

The Israelites were not in general supposed to ally themselves with "the people of the land."[142] In Joshua chapter nine, the Gibeonites go to some trouble to deceive Moses's successor into believing that they are from "a very far country" so that he will enter into alliance with them. Of course, as this was a deception it provided no yardstick for how far away a legitimate ally would have to live. The author of 1 Maccabees is consequently at pains to emphasise that the journey of Judas's envoys was "a very long journey."[143]

It was not enough, however, that Rome was distant; she must also in some sense be reliable, and righteous in her quarrels and in her government. Jeremiah,[144] Ezekiel,[145] and Hosea[146] condemned the Israelites for allying themselves with the wicked Egyptians and Assyrians, although, as Ezekiel and Joshua indicate, such alliances must be honoured once entered into. It was furthermore crucial (as implied by the de factoism of Jeremiah) that God have shown favour to the Romans by bestowing success upon their endeavours. Ezekiel had also rebuked the Israelites for the material and

---

implies that *de facto* power in itself is not to be resisted. See Benedict XV, *Celeberrima evenisse* (1919): "Nostro Predecessore di felice memoria Leone XIII . . . affermò che è dovere del cristiano la fedele sottomissione al potere costituito." (Our Predecessor of happy memory Leo XIII . . . affirmed that it is a Christian's duty faithfully to submit to the authority which is actually in power.)

[141] Goldstein, *I Maccabees*, 352.

[142] Exodus 23:32–33, 34:12; Deuteronomy 7:2.

[143] 1 Maccabees 8:19.

[144] Jeremiah 2:7; Lamentations 5:6–7.

[145] Ezekiel 16:26–29; 23:5–21

[146] Hosea 5:13; 7:11; 8:9.

moral uselessness of the alliance with Egypt;[147] the same point is made in 2 Chronicles 28:16–21 in regard to Assyria.

The Hasmoneans were reticent about the title "king." Many felt the title belonged only to the line of David. John Hyrcanus was the first to adopt the Greek *Basileus* in 110 BC. Alexander Jannaeus used the title king even in Hebrew but then abandoned it, over-striking his coins.[148] It is noteworthy that Judas's informant should implicitly praise the Romans for their mixed Republican form of government while fancying it a little more monarchical than it was. The Romans themselves, once they became aware of such discussions thanks to Panaetius and Polybius, were also rather pleased with the manner in which the wisdom of their ancestors had fashioned a constitution in equal parts monarchical, aristocratic, and politic.[149] If the first of these three turned out to be lacking, Judas's source in his imagination made up the deficiency.

It is not impossible that the sacred author sees more than mere justifiable expedience in the Roman alliance. Although most references to the coming in of the "nations" in messianic times are in the plural, not all of them are. Goldstein points out that before speaking of various nations Isaiah 55:5 speaks of one particular nation that will be called by the Lord: "Behold you shall call a nation, which you knew not: and the nations that knew not you shall run to you, because of the Lord your God." In Matthew 21:43 the Lord Himself, addressing the chief priests at the conclusion of the parable of the vineyard, uses the singular when speaking of the nation that will receive the kingdom of God: "Therefore I say to you that the kingdom of God shall be taken from you and shall be given to a nation yielding the fruits thereof." Goldstein also points out that by the magic of Hebrew,

---

[147] Ezekiel 29:6–7—an allusion, it seems, to the idiom in 2 Kings 18:21; cf. Hosea 14:4.

[148] W.D. Davies and Louis Finkelstein, eds., *The Cambridge History of Judaism,* vol. 2 (Cambridge: Cambridge University Press, 1989), 350; Goldstein, *I Maccabees*, 356.

[149] See Jonathan Powell's introduction to Cicero, *The Republic and the Laws* (Oxford: Oxford World's Classics, 1998).

Isaiah 26:11 can be made to read "Rome is Thy hand." Indeed, Goldstein interprets much of chapter eight of 1 Maccabees to be an attempt to set up an extensive parallel between the political structure and mores of the Romans and those of the Jews. He translates the opening verse as "Judas had heard of the Romans: that they were a great power who welcomed all who wished to join them and established ties of friendship with all who approached them" and comments:

> Our author wished to portray the Romans as being very similar to the Jews. Just as the Jews accept all who are willing to become full proselytes as "full citizens," so do the Romans. Just as the Jews grant friendship to all who make even a partial approach to the ways of the true God, so the Romans grant friendship to all who seek their alliance. . . . Just as Alexander Jannaeus had renounced the royal title so no Roman presumed to be king (vs. 14). Just as the Jewish elders in the Gerousia deliberated for the good order of the Jews, so did the Roman senate for the Romans (vs. 15). Just as each of the "judges" and "princes" of the Hasmonean dynasty ruled with the full consent of his subjects . . . so did the Romans submit to rule by their single (!) consul.[150]

Interestingly Augustine too in the *City of God* sees a "shadowy resemblance" between Rome founded as the universal refuge of outlaws and the Church of Christ constituted out of sinners by the forgiveness of sins.[151] Goldstein even speculates that the Jews may have seen at this point a hopeful sign in the similar sound of the Divine Name and the Roman chief deity Jove. It is hard not to be reminded of the circumstances in which

[150] Goldstein, *I Maccabees*, 347.

[151] Augustine, *City of God*, 5, 17: ". . . habet aliquid, cui per umbram quandam simile fuit asylum illud Romuleum, quo multitudinem, qua illa ciuitas conderetur, quorumlibet delictorum congregauit inpunitas."

the Hebrew kingship arose with the demand of the people for a king and God's (and Samuel's) reluctance.[152] This problem would eventfully be resolved by the fact that the hereditary king of the line of David would turn out to be the Incarnate deity Himself and live and reign forever.[153] But if the Lord is once more Himself the king of Israel, it would seem the time of the judges is restored with a non-regal limited monarchy distinct from but bound by the priesthood. This at least is St Thomas's analysis of

---

[152] 1 Samuel 8. See Alan Fimister, *Neoscholastic Humanism and the Reunification of Europe* (Brussels: Peter Lang, 2008), 76.

[153] "Yet through virtuous living man is further ordained to a higher end, which consists in the enjoyment of God, as we have said above. Consequently, since society must have the same end as the individual man, it is not the ultimate end of an assembled multitude to live virtuously, but through virtuous living to attain to the possession of God. If this end could be attained by the power of human nature, then the duty of a king would have to include the direction of men to it. We are supposing, of course, that he is called king to whom the supreme power of governing in human affairs is entrusted. Now the higher the end to which a government is ordained, the loftier that government is. Indeed, we always find that the one to whom it pertains to achieve the final end commands those who execute the things that are ordained to that end. For example, the captain, whose business it is to regulate navigation, tells the shipbuilder what kind of ship he must construct to be suitable for navigation; and the ruler of a city, who makes use of arms, tells the blacksmith what kind of arms to make. But because a man does not attain his end, which is the possession of God, by human power but by divine—according to the words of the apostle (Rom 6:23): 'By the grace of God life everlasting'—therefore the task of leading him to that last end does not pertain to human but to divine government. Consequently, government of this kind pertains to that king who is not only a man, but also God, namely, our Lord Jesus Christ, Who by making men sons of God brought them to the glory of Heaven. This then is the government which has been delivered to Him and which 'shall not be destroyed' (Dan 7:14), on account of which He is called, in Holy Writ, not Priest only, but King. As Jeremiah says (23:5): 'The king shall reign and he shall be wise.' Hence a royal priesthood is derived from Him, and what is more, all those who believe in Christ, in so far as they are His members, are called kings and priests." St Thomas Aquinas, *De Regno* 1, 15, in *On Kingship: To the King of Cyprus*, trans. Gerald B. Phelan (Toronto: Pontifical Institute of Mediaeval Studies, 1949).

the precepts of the Old Law concerning rulers (and incidentally the ideal form of government). In Question 105 of the *Prima Secundae*, he asks himself whether the Old Law contained fitting precepts concerning rulers:

> Two points are to be observed concerning the right ordering of rulers in a state or nation. One is that all should take some share in the government: for this form of constitution ensures peace among the people, commends itself to all, and is most enduring, as stated in *Polit.* ii, 6. The other point is to be observed in respect of the kinds of government, or the different ways in which the constitutions are established. For whereas these differ in kind, as the Philosopher states (*Polit.* iii, 5), nevertheless the first place is held by the "kingdom," where the power of government is vested in one; and "aristocracy," which signifies government by the best, where the power of government is vested in a few. Accordingly, the best form of government is in a state or kingdom, where one is given the power to preside over all; while under him are others having governing powers: and yet a government of this kind is shared by all, both because all are eligible to govern, and because the rulers are chosen by all. For this is the best form of polity, being partly kingdom, since there is one at the head of all; partly aristocracy, in so far as a number of persons are set in authority; partly democracy, i.e., government by the people, in so far as the rulers can be chosen from the people, and the people have the right to choose their rulers.
>
> Such was the form of government established by the Divine Law. For Moses and his successors governed the people in such a way that each of them was ruler over all; so that there was a kind of kingdom. Moreover, seventy-two men were chosen, who were elders in virtue: for it is written (Deuteronomy 1:15): "I took out of your tribes wise and honourable, and appointed them rulers": so

> that there was an element of aristocracy. But it was a democratical government in so far as the rulers were chosen from all the people; for it is written (Exodus 18:21): "Provide out of all the people wise men," etc.; and, again, in so far as they were chosen by the people; wherefore it is written (Deuteronomy 1:13): "Let me have from among you wise men," etc. Consequently it is evident that the ordering of the rulers was well provided for by the Law.[154]

St Thomas also seems to see parallels in the structure of the Roman Republic, for in Question 95 of the *Prima Secundae* he considers the various forms of human law emerging from monarchy, aristocracy, and democracy, concluding: "Finally, there is a form of government made up of all these, and which is the best: and in this respect we have law sanctioned by the 'Lords and Commons,' as stated by Isidore."[155]

Goldstein offers one final reason why the author of Maccabees might desire to emphasise the non-regal character of the Roman polity:

> Our author has more than one reason to praise Rome for being a republic. Eschatological prophesy believed by our author predicted that the kingdom of the Greeks (the Hellenistic empires beginning with Alexander's) would be followed by a fourth and last world kingdom (Dan 2:44). Jews believed that the fourth kingdom would be their own, but they were also aware of the danger of misinterpreting prophesy (cf. Dan 11:14; J. *BJ* vi 5.4.312–13). Though Rome might fulfil Num 24:24 (cf. Dan 11:30), as a republic it could not be the fourth kingdom.[156]

---

[154] *Summa theologiae*, I-II, Q. 105, art. 1.

[155] *Summa theologiae*, I-II, Q. 95, art. 4: "Est etiam aliquod regimen ex istis commixtum, quod est optimum, et secundum hoc sumitur lex, 'quam maiores natu simul cum plebibus sanxerunt,' ut Isidorus dicit."

[156] Goldstein, *I Maccabees*, 355.

If indeed Hasmonean Jews drew comfort from the fact that Rome was a republic and that they themselves still had some prospect of being the all-conquering fourth monarchy of Daniel, they were to be disappointed. Rome's republican (or at least non-monarchical) days were numbered. At the moment of its greatest triumph, the empire of the Roman people would receive the monarchical yoke seemingly broken long ago when the People of Israel were first returning from their exile in Babylon.[157] As Gibbon puts it,

---

[157] Caution is necessary here. The idea that the "republic" ceased in 27 BC is bound up with the anti-"Byzantine" bias of the Latin West, in particular with its Renaissance iteration. The emperors always remained magistrates elected by their fellow citizens and removable by the same power. Writing to the emperor in Constantinople at the end of his life, St Gregory the Great observed that "there is this difference between the kings of the nations and the emperors of the republic, that the kings of the nations are lords of slaves, but the emperors of the republic lords of freemen." The Roman emperors never took the title "Rex" because, as St Thomas reminds us, "the royal name was hateful to the Romans." Although Tiberius (supposedly on the advice of Augustus) abolished the assembly of the people in AD 14, it would still meet once in each reign in order to enact the *lex de imperio* by which the Senate and the People of Rome conferred the powers of the Republic on the *Princeps Imperator* for his lifetime.

Latin Westerners have long seen the deposition of emperors in military coups or civic riots as examples of the besetting "problem of succession" which has been resolved since the Middle Ages through the hereditary principle and latterly through a free and fair electoral cycle. Anthony Kaldelis has recently shown that this was not how the classical Romans or the later "Byzantines" saw the matter at all. They saw these episodes instead as legitimate exercises of a right of recall by the sovereign people over the first of their magistrates. St Thomas concurs that this is a legitimate act: "If to provide itself with a king belongs to the right of a given multitude, it is not unjust that the king be deposed or have his power restricted by that same multitude if, becoming a tyrant, he abuses the royal power. It must not be thought that such a multitude is acting unfaithfully in deposing the tyrant, even though it had previously subjected itself to him in perpetuity, because he himself has deserved that the covenant with his subjects should not be kept, since, in ruling the multitude, he did not act faithfully as the office of a king demands."

This was precisely what the Byzantines thought they were doing when they acclaimed a new emperor in opposition to a tyrant. They even used the same terms

"The arms of the republic, sometimes vanquished in battle, always victorious in war, advanced with rapid steps to the Euphrates, the Danube, the Rhine, and the Ocean; and the images of gold, or silver, or brass, that might serve to represent the nations and their kings, were successively broken by the iron monarchy of Rome."[158]

The historian of the Roman empire refers of course to the vision of Daniel,[159] the same vision which exercised the hopes and curiosities of the Jewish people in the age of Judas Maccabaeus and afterwards. For the direct references[160] to the Romans in the books of the Maccabees are

---

for electing and deposing bishops and emperors alike: "Axios!" and "Anaxios!" In the light of St Thomas's comment in his commentary on 2 Thessalonians that the Roman empire has not perished but passed from the temporal to the spiritual sphere, it is striking that the patristic method of electing bishops—still upheld, in theory, by the Gregorian reform movement of the eleventh century—is identical to the Roman/Byzantine Constitution as analysed by Kaldelis. Even Gibbon admitted that "the subjects of Rome enjoyed in the church the privilege which they had lost in the republic, of choosing the magistrates whom they were bound to obey." Kaldelis would argue that, at least in regard to the *highest* magistrate of New Rome, they had not lost it at all.

158 Edward Gibbon, *The Decline of Fall of the Roman Empire*, vol. 4 (London: Everyman, 1993), 119.

159 And, it seems, to the frontiers of the Messianic kingdom as prophesied in Psalm 71:8, "And he shall rule from sea to sea, and from the river unto the ends of the earth"; cf. Psalm 89:25 and Zechariah 9:10. George Berkeley sees the "sea to sea" element fulfilled in the evangelization of the Americas: "Westward the Course of Empire takes its Way; The four first Acts already past, A fifth shall close the Drama with the Day; Time's noblest Offspring is the last" (*America or The Muse's Refuge: A Prophecy*). Even more explicit are Katherine Lee Bates's *America the Beautiful*, which ends with the line "from sea to shining sea," and the motto of Canada, "A Mari Usque Ad Mare," which is a direct citation of Psalm 71:8 in the Vulgate. The Americas were traversed and the Pacific sighted in 1513 and they were subjected to the sovereignty of the last pontifically crowned Holy Roman Emperor, Charles V, in the ensuing decades.

160 We will not consider here the word *Kittim* (םיִתִּכ,) which appears at Genesis 10:4; Numbers 24:24; 1 Chronicles 1:7; Jeremiah 2:10; and Ezekiel 27:6, and which is translated

not the only or the most important references in the Old Testament. The Fathers (with the sole exception of Ephraim the Syrian)[161] are clear that the Book of Daniel is rich with prophetic references to Rome and her empire. These passages are of enormous importance as they are key to the understanding of the figure of the Son of Man, the favoured term by which the Lord referred to Himself. The Lord Himself made clear the centrality of the Book of Daniel in the most eloquent possible way by quoting the words of Daniel 7:13 in answer to the High Priest's question "Are you the Christ, the Son of the Blessed God?"

Matthew 26:64

> σὺ εἶπας: πλὴν λέγω ὑμῖν, ἀπ' ἄρτι ὄψεσθε τὸν υἱὸν τοῦ ἀνθρώπου καθήμενον ἐκ δεξιῶν τῆς δυνάμεως καὶ ἐρχόμενον ἐπὶ τῶν νεφελῶν τοῦ οὐρανοῦ.[162]
>
> You have said it. Nevertheless I say to you, hereafter you shall see the Son of man sitting on the right hand of the power of God and coming in the clouds of heaven.

---

in the LXX at Daniel 11:30 as "Romans" (Ρωμαιοι). In general, the term seems in the Pentateuch to have been specific to some region in Asia Minor or the Aegean and later on to have become a general term for Westerners.

161 J.A. Assemani, ed., *Sancti patris nostri Ephraem Syri Opera omnia* (Rome, 1737). The sixth-century Nestorian monk Cosmas Indicopleustes, author of *The Christian Topography*, interestingly agrees with Ephrem. He divides the Medes and the Persians into two different monarchies and makes the Macedonians the fourth (see below). The effect of this, however, is to make the Romans the fifth monarchy without qualification and to exalt the empire even more than the orthodox fathers. Cosmas Indicopleustes, *The Christian Topography of Cosmas, an Egyptian Monk: Translated from the Greek, and Edited with Notes and Introduction* (Cambridge: Cambridge University Press, 2010), 2.75, pp. 69–71.

162 E. and E. Nestle and B. and K. Aland, *Novum Testamentum Graece et Latine* (Stuttgart: Deutsche Bibelgesellschaft, 2008), 79.

Mark 14:62

> ἐγώ εἰμι, καὶ ὄψεσθε τὸν υἱὸν τοῦ ἀνθρώπου ἐκ δεξιῶν καθήμενον τῆς δυνάμεως καὶ ἐρχόμενον μετὰ τῶν νεφελῶν τοῦ οὐρανοῦ.[163]
>
> I am. And you shall see the Son of man sitting on the right hand of the power of God and coming with the clouds of heaven.

This was the climactic question of Jesus's trial, and the answer which led directly to His passion and death. Here it is that the Lord chooses to reveal the significance of the mysterious title which He had used of himself throughout His public ministry. He is the heavenly being of Daniel chapter seven Who founds the fifth and final monarchy of salvation history and reigns forever:

Daniel 7:13 (LXX)

> ἐθεώρουν ἐν ὁράματι τῆς νυκτὸς καὶ ἰδοὺ ἐπὶ τῶν νεφελῶν τοῦ οὐρανοῦ ὡς υἱὸς ἀνθρώπου ἤρχετο[164]
>
> One like the Son of man came with the clouds of heaven, and he came even to the ancient of days . . .
>
> . . . and they presented him before him. (v. 14) And he gave him power, and glory, and a kingdom: and all peoples, tribes, and tongues shall serve him: his power is an everlasting power that shall not be taken away: and his kingdom that shall not be destroyed.

Given this as well as the peculiar importance of the title "Son of Man" to the Lord Himself, the importance of grasping the meaning of the prophesy of Daniel 7 can hardly be overemphasised.

---

163 Nestle/Aland, *Novum Testamentum*, 141.

164 A. Rahlfs and R. Hanhart, *Septuaginta* (Stuttgart: Deutsche Bibelgesellschaft, 2006), 913–14.

The Book of the Prophet Daniel contains two prophecies which, it seems clear, are intended to describe in symbolic language the same sequence of events. The first occurs right at the beginning of the book and is originally a prophecy received by King Nebuchadnezzar of Babylon in the form of a dream. He demands the interpretation of this dream from his wise men but refuses to tell the content of the dream itself (presumably to guard against false or self-serving claims to interpret it). The sages of Babylon are unable to tell the king the meaning of the dream and he decrees their execution. Daniel and his companions are taken up in the decree even though they are not themselves aware of the original request. Daniel prays for the gift of interpretation and for inspiration as to the content of the dream. God reveals this to him and he duly informs Nebuchadnezzar of the content and meaning of his dream. Nebuchadnezzar is suitably impressed and makes various declarations concerning the power and wisdom of Daniel's god.

The dream (to which we shall return) concerned a statue the head and shoulders of which symbolised Nebuchadnezzar's own monarchy. Surprisingly the king reacts to this incident by building a huge golden statue of himself and demanding that all his various officials and other subjects worship the statue. The Jews who do not do this are denounced, and Daniel's three companions are cast into a terrible fiery furnace for their refusal. They evince no fear but trust in God and are preserved from harm even in the flames themselves. Nebuchadnezzar once more declares his admiration for their god.

The next chapter of Daniel reads as a decree of Nebuchadnezzar himself in which he describes another dream which he had and the interpretation of it, again given by Daniel. It prophesies the madness of Nebuchadnezzar for a sevenfold period (of what is not clear) and then his restoration and conversion.

That, it would seem, is the end of Nebuchadnezzar, for the book now moves on to the incident of one of Nebuchadnezzar's successors, Belshazzar, who decides to hold a feast using the vessels plundered from the Temple in Jerusalem. A mysterious hand appears and writes an inscription on the wall which (Daniel explains to the king) indicates the imminent destruction of his monarchy.

Chapter six concerns King Darius the Mede who reigns afterwards. Inspired by envious rivals of Daniel, he commands that anyone offering petition to anyone, god or man, other than the king for the next thirty days should be thrown to the lions. Daniel carries on praying to the Lord and is (much to the king's regret) cast to the lions. The lions do not eat him and Darius breaks forth into praises of Daniel's god.

The chronological sequence is then interrupted and chapter seven relates a vision which Daniel had in the reign of Belshazzar, the vision which Jesus quotes to the High Priest at his trial.

This is followed by another (later) vision which also occurred in the reign of Belshazzar, and which is explicitly said by the Angel Gabriel to describe the war between the Medio-Persian kingdom and that of the Greeks.

Then, in the first year of Darius, Daniel prays to be enlightened concerning the meaning of the prophesy of Jeremiah that the exile in Babylon will last seventy years. Gabriel appears and informs him that this prophesy in fact refers to a period of 490 years (seventy weeks of years). This is strange given that, as we have seen, the seventy years were fulfilled literally.[165]

It would be tempting to suppose that there must be a symbolic connection between the literal period of seventy years during which Judah was compelled to "serve the king of Babylon" (either as described by the Book of Daniel or more generally) and the seventy weeks of years from 457 BC to AD 26, but such a mammoth exegetical task is beyond the

[165] Josephus, *Antiquities* 10.11.1, in *Josephus: The Complete Works*, 224–25. Nebuchadnezzar deported exiles even before he became king (including, as it happens, Daniel) in 605 BC, which, counting inclusively, yields seventy years.

present project.[166] However, more germane to our purpose, there are hints among the Fathers of a parallel between the events of Daniel 2–5 and the period elapsing between the destruction of the Temple in AD 70 and the conversion of the Roman empire in the fourth century. Indeed, St Luke himself appears to be drawing such parallels in Acts 28:30 which bares strong similarities and some pointed differences to 2 Kings 25:30. The statue of Daniel 2 is in some sense both a symbol of the temporal power and a statue of Nebuchadnezzar, such that Babylon and Nebuchadnezzar alike are symbols of the temporal power. The drama would seem to require that the symbolism be particularly close in that era in which the sovereign who is symbolised by the head lives and reigns and when the era symbolised by the legs of iron and feet of clay is underway. Meanwhile, 1 Peter 5:13 and Revelation 17:9 appear to apply the name Babylon to Rome directly.

Augustine asserts this point explicitly in his famous (ninety-third) Letter to Vincentius:

> Truly, if past events recorded in the prophetic books were figures of the future, there was given under King Nebuchadnezzar a figure both of the time which the Church had under the apostles, and of that which she has now. In the age of the apostles and martyrs, that was fulfilled which was prefigured when the aforesaid king compelled pious and just men to bow down to his image, and cast into the flames all who refused. Now, however, is fulfilled that which

[166] For 490 years, the people did not observe the sabbatical rest for the land that was decreed in the law (see Exodus 23:10–11; Leviticus 25:4; cf. 2 Chronicles 36:21), resulting in seventy missing sabbatical years. As a result, the people were deported for seventy years, but, since they had offended for 490 years, the kingdom was not restored until that period of time had elapsed. The first period must be served before the people can return to the land, while the second must be served before the monarchy of David can be restored.

> was prefigured soon after in the same king, when, being converted to the worship of the true God, he made a decree throughout his empire, that whosoever should speak against the God of Shadrach, Meshach, and Abednego, should suffer the penalty which their crime deserved. The earlier time of that king represented the former age of emperors who did not believe in Christ, at whose hands the Christians suffered because of the wicked; but the later time of that king represented the age of the successors to the imperial throne, now believing in Christ, at whose hands the wicked suffer because of the Christians.[167]

It would seem reasonable on this basis to identify Nebuchadnezzar's golden statue and persecution of the three young men as a type of the Flavian misinterpretation of the oracle concerning the world rulers to emerge from Judea at the end of the sixties AD and the subsequent persecution of the Church. In the fourth century, Porphyry, the polemical anti-Christian pupil of Plotinus and ideological cheerleader for the Great Persecution, expounded at length on the fraudulent character of the prophesies of Daniel.[168] They were, he insisted, written after the event and referred not to the empires of the Babylonians, Persians, Macedonians, and Romans but to the empires of the Babylonians, Medes, Persians, and Macedonians. Of the Fathers of the Church, only Ephrem the Syrian (without conceding the *post-factum* claim) agreed with Porphyry's exegesis. Modern exegetes have tended to agree with Ephrem (or rather, one suspects, with Porphyry). This can hardly be much more than ideological prejudice given the timescale in chapter nine and the supremely apposite description of the Macedonians (if they are the third beast) as a leopard with four wings and four heads. Alexander the Great conquered the known world in ten years and

---

[167] St Augustine, *Letter* 93:9 (PL 33:325), trans. J.G. Cunningham, in *NPNF* I, vol. 1 (Buffalo, NY: Christian Literature Publishing Co., 1887).

[168] Hartman and Di Lella, *Book of Daniel*.

then died, leaving his realm to be divided between four of his generals.[169] Furthermore, in the very next chapter the Medes and the Persians are explicitly treated as a single empire and the Macedonian kingdom is shown as a he-goat with one horn subsequently replaced by four horns.

The attribution of the posture and mind of a man to the first beast appears to be a relatively clear reference to the conversion of Nebuchadnezzar.[170] Indeed, this is an important indication that in the language of Daniel (and Revelation), a "beast" is a pagan polity or its head while a "man" is a polity or its head rightly ordered to God. Hippolytus attributes the ribs in the mouth of the bear to the kingdoms of the Persians, Medes, and Babylonians in the power of the second beast,[171] and the command to "devour much flesh" to the attempted extermination of the Jews recorded in Esther.[172] The symbolism of the third beast has already been expounded.

The Book then once more interrupts the chronological order (assuming Darius the Mede is Darius the Great) and in chapter nine reports a vision of Daniel "in the first year of Darius the son of Ahasuerus," which is that referred to earlier, affording the exact dating of the Messiah's public ministry. The remaining predictions in the book seem to pertain to the end times or in more detail to the persecution of Antiochus Epiphanes, and so do not touch directly upon this investigation.

Having examined the references to Rome in the Old Testament, it behoves us to examine their fulfilment in the New.

---

169 Jerome, *Commentary on Daniel*, 7.6, in Gleason L. Archer, *Jerome's Commentary on Daniel* (Eugene, OR: Wipf & Stock, 2009), 75.

170 Hippolytus, "On Christ and Antichrist" (PG 10:745), trans. J.H. MacMahon, in *ANF*, vol. 5 (Buffalo, NY: Christian Literature Publishing Co., 1886), 209.

171 Hippolytus, *Scholia on Daniel* (PG 10:681), trans. S.D.F. Salmond, in *ANF*, vol. 5 (Buffalo, NY: Christian Literature Publishing Co., 1886), 189; Jerome, *Commentary on Daniel*, 74 (PL 25:529–30).

172 Jerome, *Commentary on Daniel*, 74–75 (PL 25:529).

4

Why the Church Is Roman: Fulfilment

The gulf which yawns in the Protestant Holy Book between the last of the minor prophets and the beginning of the Gospel according to St Matthew does not trouble the authentic canon of Sacred Scripture. Nevertheless, there is indeed a hiatus of a little over a century between the High Priesthood of John Hyrcanus and the appearance of the Archangel Gabriel to St Zachariah in the sanctuary of the Temple. In this interval, Rome's relationship to the Jewish people was transformed utterly from that of a promising ally to that of a sponsor of a brutal Idumean usurper and, shortly, occupier of the Promised Land. Jacob had prophesied in the first age of the chosen race that "the sceptre shall not be taken away from Judah, nor a ruler from his thigh, till he come that is to be sent, and he shall be the expectation of nations."[173] Although no member of the male line of Judah had reigned in Jerusalem since the destruction of the Temple in 586 BC, the Hasmonean Dynasty which led the revolt described in the last two books of the Old Testament and reigned over Israel thereafter were descended from Elisheba of Judah, the wife of Aaron.[174] In Herod, for the first time someone ruled the Promised Land claiming to be king of the Jews who did not spring from the loins of Judah.[175]

[173] Genesis 49:10.

[174] Exodus 6:23.

[175] This is observed *inter alia* by Eusebius, *Hist. Eccl.* 1:6.

And yet, we have no inspired text indicating the proper response to this transformation. Is the faithful adherent of the God of Israel gloomily to accept the verdict of Providence and await a better time unless and until the pagan ruler seeks to elicit disloyalty to the law? This would seem to be the teaching of the prophets.[176] The question of where the line is to be drawn between the acceptance of the verdict of Providence and armed resistance to idolatry is most dramatically raised by the question of the coinage. This arises in the context of the payment of tribute and the changing of money.

These passages are often taken in isolation, which obscures several of their vital resonances. The conversation about the payment of tribute to Caesar occurs on the Tuesday of Holy Week, the triumphal entry having occurred on Sunday and the cleansing of the Temple on the Monday (Mark 11:12; 11:20). The succession of days is only apparent from a comparison of the various accounts. Monday of Holy Week is interesting in that only four events are recorded as occurring then: the first cursing of the fig tree ("May no one ever eat fruit from you again"), the cleansing of the Temple, the healing of the blind and the lame in the Temple, and a dispute with the chief priests and the scribes over children acclaiming Christ in the Temple with the words "Hosanna to the Son of David!" (Mt 21:12–17; Mk 11:12–19; Lk 19:45–46). Apart from these, the only miracles Jesus seems to have performed in Holy Week[177] were the withering of the fig tree and the healing of Malchus's ear.

It is possible that Luke's account of Jesus weeping over Jerusalem might be properly placed on the Monday as well. However, because Luke is not clear about the night intervening between the triumphal entry and the cleansing of the Temple, it is hard to be sure. The passage is interesting as it is immediately prefaced by the remark (which does belong to the Sunday)

[176] See above, note 140.

[177] Aside from the institution of the Holy Eucharist and those associated with the Passion itself, e.g., the darkening of the sun.

"I tell you, if these were silent, the very stones would cry out" (Luke 19:40). Given the importance of the motif of stones being transformed into men for the understanding of the later passages, it is worth examining Jesus's lament over the Holy City:

> And when he drew near and saw the city he wept over it, saying, "Would that even today you knew the things that make for peace! But now they are hid from your eyes. For the days shall come upon you, when your enemies will cast up a bank about you and surround you, and hem you in on every side, and dash you to the ground, you and your children within you, and they will not leave one stone upon another in you; because you did not know the time of your visitation."[178]

The ensuing chronology is clear from all three synoptics. The morning after the cleansing of the Temple (Tuesday), Jesus returned to Jerusalem cursing the fig tree for a second time ("May no fruit ever come from you again!") and instantaneously withering it. The Lord then echoes His saying of Matthew 17:20 about the ability of faith the size a mustard seed to move mountains (see also Luke 17:6), telling the disciples:

> Have faith in God. Truly, I say to you, whoever says to this mountain, "Be taken up and cast into the sea," and does not doubt in his heart, but believes that what he says will come to pass, it will be done for him. Therefore I tell you, whatever you ask in prayer, believe that you have received it, and it will be yours.[179]

The echo of the comment about faith the size of a mustard seed is not insignificant given the verbal parallels between the parable of the mustard seed (Mt 13:31–32; Mk 4:30–32; Lk 13:18–19) and the second dream

---

[178] Luke 19:41–44.

[179] Mark 11:22–24.

of Nebuchadnezzar (Daniel 4).[180] The withering of the fig tree is clearly a sort of acted parable relating back to the actual parable Jesus gave some months earlier, as recorded in Luke 13:6–9:[181]

> A man had a fig tree planted in his vineyard; and he came seeking fruit on it and found none. And he said to the vinedresser, "Lo, these three years I have come seeking fruit on this fig tree, and I find none. Cut it down; why should it use up the ground?" And he answered him, "Let it alone, sir, this year also, till I dig about it and put on manure. And if it bears fruit next year, well and good; but if not, you can cut it down."

Given the obvious parallels with the duration of Jesus's public ministry, it seems probable that the fig tree here represents the Jewish commonwealth while the withering of an actual fig tree on the Tuesday of Holy Week alludes to the imminent transfer of the covenant and to the doom of the "scoffers who rule this people in Jerusalem." This suggestion is reinforced by the words "this mountain" (Mark 11:23), which presumably refer to the Temple Mount. The implication is that the Temple Mount will be

---

[180] In Daniel 4, the vision of Nebuchadnezzar—of a great tree which fills the whole earth and gives shelter to the beasts of the field and the birds of the air—cannot help but recall the parable of the mustard seed in Matthew (13:31–32), Mark (4:30–32), and Luke (13:18–19). Nevertheless, there are crucial differences. The tree of Babylon shelters both the birds of the air and the beasts of the field together, unlike the tree of the parable which shelters only the birds of the air. It is surely not unreasonable to detect here a reference to the coexistence of the faithful and unbelievers in the temporal commonwealth. More dramatically, the tree of Nebuchadnezzar is felled and the trunk bound with iron and bronze, symbolising the madness of the king and then his eventual conversion. Given the symbolism of iron and bronze elsewhere in Daniel, it is hard not to see here a reference to Greek philosophy and Roman jurisprudence through which the fourth monarchy is perpetuated down to the era of the Antichrist.

[181] As observed by Jakob van Bruggen, *Christ on Earth: The Gospel Narratives as History* (Grand Rapids, MI: Baker Books, 1998).

swept away overwhelmed by waters, replaced by "a foundation stone, a tested stone, a precious cornerstone, of a sure foundation," and that "by men of strange lips and with an alien tongue the LORD will speak to this people," as predicted in Isaiah 28:11–19. This passage (and for that matter Matthew 16:18) seems to allude to a tradition that Mount Zion blocks the gates of Sheol from which the waters of the flood (Genesis 7:11 and 8:2) came forth. This tradition also provides a hermeneutical key to Isaiah 11:9 and Ezekiel 47:1–12 which predict the transformation of these waters into a fresh and life-giving torrent.

Jesus now enters the Temple and (in all three synoptics) enters into a dispute over the origin of John's authority. This dispute, as the immediate sequel of the previous day's cleansing of the Temple, is also noteworthy, as John had said to "many of the Pharisees and Sadducees coming for baptism":

> You brood of vipers! Who warned you to flee from the wrath to come? Bear fruit that befits repentance, and do not presume to say to yourselves, "We have Abraham as our father"; for I tell you, God is able from these stones to raise up children to Abraham. Even now the axe is laid to the root of the trees; every tree therefore that does not bear good fruit is cut down and thrown into the fire. I baptize you with water for repentance, but he who is coming after me is mightier than I, whose sandals I am not worthy to carry; he will baptize you with the Holy Spirit and with fire. His winnowing fork is in his hand, and he will clear his threshing floor and gather his wheat into the granary, but the chaff he will burn with unquenchable fire.[182]

Given the Old Testament passages to which the events of these days have already directed us, this speech of John the Baptist is enormously important. Christ has only that morning symbolically withered the fruitless

[182] Matthew 3:7–12.

tree, comparing His action to the casting of the Temple Mount into the sea. The Messiah in Isaiah 11:8, soon to fill the world with the knowledge of the Lord as the waters cover the sea, standing on the "Holy Mountain," reaches into the serpent's den. The Temple Mount[183] is both the place where Abraham was to have sacrificed his son and the threshing floor of Ornan the Jebusite.

The previous day, reenacting the inauguration of his public ministry, Christ drove off the money changers and merchants from the threshing floor. The first year of his public ministry He had objected only to the nature of the activities undertaken there (John 2:16);[184] now He specifically objects to their obstruction of the worship of the Gentiles: "Is it not written, 'My house shall be called a house of prayer for all the nations'? But you have made it a den of robbers."[185] It is therefore extremely important that the Messiah should now vindicate the authority of John the Forerunner whose prophesies He is fulfilling. In Matthew 21:28–32, Jesus prefaces the great Parable of the Vineyard with a little parable also about a vineyard which ostensibly contrasts the attitude of repentant tax collectors and harlots to the hard-hearted chief priests and elders of the people. The parable also seems to contain an allusion to the earlier parable of the prodigal son,[186] in which not a few have seen some reference to the Jews and the Gentiles.[187] Like the repentant tax collectors and harlots, the Gentiles start badly but are saved by the grace and truth that come through Jesus Christ, while the Jews adhering to the Law are lost because, trusting in their own justice,

[183] 1 Chronicles 21:1–22:1 and 2 Chronicles 3:1.

[184] See below (pp. 88ff.) on Revelation 13.

[185] Mark 11:17; Matthew 21:13; Luke 19:46.

[186] Luke 15:11–32.

[187] E.g., Cyril of Alexandria, *A Commentary on the Gospel according to St Luke*, trans. R. Payne Smith (Oxford: Oxford University Press, 1859), Homily 107, pp. 500–505; Peter Chrysologus, *Sermon* 5, in *Selected Sermons*, ed. George E. Ganss (Washington, DC: Catholic University of America Press, 1953), 43–51.

they cannot fulfil it. The parable of the two brothers and the vineyard thus performs a double service, vindicating John the Baptist and establishing the context for the dramatic teaching of the parable that follows.

In the great parable of the vineyard, Christ reveals to the rulers of the people in Jerusalem God's plan to raise up children to Abraham from the stones, a plan in which Moriah will be uprooted and replaced by the immovable faith of Peter. All three synoptics place this parable in this key chronological position—the morning after the cleansing of the Temple and immediately before the question about tribute to Caesar. God has established Israel as His vineyard. He has sent for the fruits via His servants the prophets, whom the tenants have beaten, wounded, murdered and stoned. Finally, He has sent His beloved Son. Reprising the theme of the desire to establish justice without grace, the tenants imagine that if they murder the heir they will have the vineyard for themselves, and so they kill the owner's beloved son:

> "When therefore the owner of the vineyard comes, what will he do to those tenants?" They said to him, "He will put those wretches to a miserable death, and let out the vineyard to other tenants who will give him the fruits in their seasons." Jesus said to them, "Have you never read in the scriptures: 'The very stone which the builders rejected has become the head of the corner; this was the Lord's doing, and it is marvellous in our eyes'? Therefore I tell you, the kingdom of God will be taken away from you and given to a nation producing the fruits of it."[188]

Thus the stones transformed into children of Abraham now have a living cornerstone: the Messiah. And the new tenants of the Lord's vineyard—"the people of the prince who is to come"—have a name: the Romans.

[188] Matthew 21:41–43.

Matthew tells us[189] that the Lord also recounted at this time the parable of the wedding feast in a version which strongly emphasizes the reference to the destruction of Jerusalem in AD 70 and parallels the legend of Romulus's establishment of the city of Rome through the recruitment of brigands. Furthermore, in describing the Romans' destruction of Jerusalem in this third parable, Christ, like Daniel before Him, refers to the Roman armies as God's own: "and he sent *his* troops and destroyed those murderers and burned their city."

There is a splendid irony in the passage with which Luke, who, like Mark, moves straight from the parable of the vineyards to the question about tribute, connects the two episodes.

> The scribes and the chief priests tried to lay hands on him at that very hour, but they feared the people; for they perceived that he had told this parable against them. So they watched him, and sent spies, who pretended to be sincere, that they might take hold of what he said, so as to deliver him up to the authority and jurisdiction of the governor.[190]

Their intention is to deliver the Messiah to the authority and jurisdiction of the governor, in the sense of bringing it about that the Roman procurator will be the one to cut Him off. What they do not realize is that thereby they will bring it about that the Romans will become the Messiah's people.[191]

Before examining the tribute passage, a crucial element in the cleansing of the Temple must be considered. The reason the pilgrims approaching the sanctuary needed to change their money (the location of which activity aroused the wrath of Christ) was that the coinage they employed for everyday transactions could not be taken into the Temple because it bore upon its face the graven image of Caesar, who claimed on the inscription

[189] Matthew 22:1–14.

[190] Luke 20:19–20.

[191] See also John 11:48, "If we let him alone so, all will believe in him; and the Romans will come, and take away our place (τόπον) and nation."

of the coins to be the son of [a] god, one who permitted (and would soon demand) that his image be worshiped.[192] The coins were thus an abomination which could not be taken into the Holy Place. The very fact that the exchange into the non-idolatrous currency of the Temple occurred in the court of the Gentiles was a most eloquent denial that the court of the Gentiles belonged to the Temple and thus a rejection of God's plan to extend His covenant to all the nations.

And yet this entire transaction was mired in hypocrisy because the half-shekel in which transactions within the Temple "proper" were to be conducted and the Temple tax paid bore the likeness of Hercules/Baal, the god of Tyre. It was the coins of this false god that were minted by a special mint created for this purpose in the Holy Land.[193] The Roman authorities were willing that the Jews have a special coinage for their Temple but not that it be seen as a totem of sovereignty, and so they insisted that it be minted in an existing (or rather historic) non-Jewish form. The half-shekel tax was demanded by the Torah.[194] Yet the Temple authorities were unwilling to accept the Roman currency not because of its possibly idolatrous character (although after the revolt in 66 a new currency without images of sensitive creatures would be minted) but because of its lower silver purity. Thus, Caesar was left in the court of the Gentiles while Hercules/Baal was taken into the interior of the Temple and stored in the treasury. Most likely it was in this coin that the betrayer was rendered the thirty coins for his service. There is even a surviving rabbinical edict which decrees that only this coin was acceptable as payment in the Temple.[195]

---

[192] Suetonius, *[The Works of] Suetonius*, trans. John Carew Rolfe (Cambridge, MA: Harvard University Press, 1998); Philo, *[The Works of] Philo*, vol. 10, trans. Francis Henry Colson (Cambridge, MA: Harvard University Press, 1962).

[193] Christopher Howgego, Volker Heuchert, and Andrew Burnett, eds., *Coinage and Identity in the Roman Provinces* (Oxford: Oxford University Press, 2005), 164–65.

[194] Exodus 30:11–16.

[195] Mishnah Bekhorot 8:7; Babylonian Talmud Kiddushin 11a.

Christ's protest against the money changers, in the form it took in the last year of His public ministry, is thus highly charged, when we consider that it was the taking of the abomination of desolation[196] into the Temple that justified the abandonment by the Maccabees of the prophetic stance of passive submission to their pagan rulers. The implications of Christ's identification of the court of the Gentiles as an integral part of the Temple and consequent objection to the presence of the money changers there might be politically explosive.

The tension implied in this act can hardly have been defused by the second and third of the parables He had just delivered in the Temple, with their promises that the covenant will be removed and the city destroyed. It is therefore quite logical from a tactical perspective that the scribes and the chief priests, the Pharisees and the Herodians should seek at this moment to entangle Him in an overt revolutionary statement against the Roman authorities.

The coalition of enemies the Lord has ranged against Himself is impressive, confirming the Augustinian intuition of the essentially binary character of the human race.[197] This grand coalition of the enemies of God, more than usually united to their fallen prince, speaks with the authentic voice of the tempter flattering the Messiah for very fact of His alienation from all factions of the world. As Matthew has it, "Teacher, we know that you are true, and teach the way of God truthfully, and care for no man; for you do not regard the position of men. Tell us, then, what you think. Is it lawful to pay taxes to Caesar, or not?" The Lord is not disposed to play the game. "Jesus, aware of their malice, said, 'Why put me to the test, you hypocrites?'"

The dilemma constructed by the Lord's enemies is intended to work as follows: If Christ admits the lawfulness of paying tax to Caesar, He presumably alienates the nationalist constituency His enemies falsely

196 Daniel 11:31.

197 Endorsed by Leo XIII in the 1884 Encyclical *Humanum Genus*.

suppose Him to have been cultivating by the cleansing of the Temple; if He condemns the payment of taxes to Caesar, He makes an assertion for which the authorities can be induced to execute Him.

Of course, the real purpose of the Lord's cleansing of the Temple was precisely what He said it was: to remove from the part of the Temple reserved for the worship of the Gentiles profane activities which implied the exclusion of the nations from the worship of the one true God. It was certainly not to provide the *casus belli* for a revolt against the Romans. Rather it foreshadowed the sending down of the Spirit to convert those very Romans from their idolatry to the worship of the God of Israel. The idolatrous coins were brought into the outer court not by the Romans but by the Temple authorities who, by their rejection of the Messiah, were soon to bring upon themselves and into the precincts of the Temple far more violent and terrible trophies of the false gods of Latium than a few imperial *denarii*. As for the restoration by war of the kingdom of Israel, the Lord would, by means of that very rejection, abolish the Old Law with its temporal rewards and promises a mere four days hence.[198]

By His answer to their challenge Christ directs His interlocutors' attention back to the true issue at stake in the events of the previous day: idolatry. He summons a coin for His inspection. As with the incident of the Temple tax,[199] Christ does not appear to carry any money Himself. He calls for a coin and it is shown to Him. He asks:

> "Whose likeness and inscription has it?" They said, "Caesar's." He said to them, "Then render to Caesar the things that are Caesar's, and to God the things that are God's." And they were not able in the presence of the people to catch him by what he said; but marvelling at his answer they were silent.[200]

---

[198] Pius XII, *Mystici Corporis Christi* §29–30.

[199] Matthew 17:24–27.

[200] Luke 20:24–26.

As with the inquiry about divorce,[201] Jesus brings the question back to the beginning. Man is created in the image of God and those ransomed from among men are shortly to receive the name of God Incarnate as their own;[202] the coin bears the image and the name of Caesar. Let that which is Caesar's, that is, the token denoting the goods and services available for a consideration within the "authority and jurisdiction" of Caesar, be returned to him; and that which belongs to God—man himself and all that is his—be returned to God. Yet the Temple authorities do not receive man himself and all that is his on behalf of the Lord of Israel; they receive shekels, specially minted for their benefit, with the head of Baal on one side and (ironically given their fate forty years hence) an eagle on the other. The implications were clear: the Temple authorities were idolaters—the question of the Romans was academic.

Later that day, the question of the ensigns of Roman paganism and the stones of the Temple was raised again by the disciples. "And as he came out of the Temple, one of his disciples said to him, 'Look, Teacher, what wonderful stones and what wonderful buildings!' And Jesus said to him, 'Do you see these great buildings? There will not be left here one stone upon another, that will not be thrown down.'"[203] Jesus then proceeds to expound upon the nature of the end both of Jerusalem and of the world

201 Matthew 19:3–9; Mark 10:2–12.

202 Matthew 10:22; Mark 13:13; Luke 21:17; Revelation 3:12; 14:1.

203 Mark 13:1–2 and Matthew 24:1–2; 21:5–6.

in the Eschatological Discourse. The difficulty of disentangling these two ends, typologically united as early as the Sermon on the Mount,[204] is notorious.[205] Of particular interest is the "abomination of desolation," mentioned in both Matthew 24:15 and Mark 13:14, and explicitly said in Matthew to be that to which the prophet Daniel referred.

There are three references to the abomination of desolation in Daniel.[206] It would appear that the first refers to the destruction of the Temple in AD 70, the second to the erecting of a statue of Zeus in the Temple by Antiochus Epiphanes in 167 BC, and the third to the persecution of the Antichrist.[207] The reference to "the wing of abominations" in Daniel 9:27 and the fact that where Matthew and Mark refer to the abomination of desolation Luke speaks of "Jerusalem surrounded by armies" plus the references in Matthew 24:28 and Luke 17:37 to the gathering of eagles around the corpse leads one to suspect that the sign for the fleeing of the Christians from Judea was the arrival of the Roman (eagle) standards. The appearance of Vespasian's legions and their standards, which would ultimately be worshiped by the Roman soldiers amidst the ruins of the sanctuary, was the signal for the early Christians to flee Judea.

In the event, the charges brought against Jesus by the chief priests were a distortion of His remarks made during the original cleansing of the Temple recorded in John 2:19: "Destroy this temple, and in three days I will raise it up." Redacted as a promise to destroy the Temple Himself, this claim could be presented as both a grave sacrilege and a public order offense that might interest the Romans in an execution. Unfortunately, the witnesses could not be made to agree and Caiaphas was compelled to

[204] Matthew 5:18.

[205] See, e.g., St Augustine, *Letter* 199:25 to Hesychius (PL 33:904–25), in *Letters*, vol. 4, trans. W. Parsons (New York: Fathers of the Church, 1955), 375–76.

[206] Daniel 9:27; 11:31; 12:11.

[207] Charles Arminjon, *The End of the Present World and the Mysteries of Future Life* (Manchester, NH: Sophia Institute Press, 2008).

adopt the more dangerous procedure of demanding that the Lord plainly assert His messianic dignity—something which could scarcely be an offense if true, only marginally if false, but which would interest the Romans either way. Instead Jesus asserted His divinity: "ὁ δὲ Ἰησοῦς εἶπεν: ἐγώ εἰμι, καὶ ὄψεσθε τὸν υἱὸν τοῦ ἀνθρώπου ἐκ δεξιῶν καθήμενον τῆς δυνάμεως καὶ ἐρχόμενον μετὰ τῶν νεφελῶν τοῦ οὐρανοῦ."[208]

This statement could be presented to the Romans as a claim to kingship while constituting in the sight of the Sanhedrin a blasphemous claim to divinity. It was consequently ideal for Caiaphas's purposes. What it indicates to us, as has been observed, is the centrality of Daniel and the fate of the fourth monarchy to the understanding of Christ and the fifth monarchy. After a second and rather more regular[209] hearing in the morning, recorded by Luke, in while Christ obligingly almost exactly repeated the crucial statement of the night before (for which there were now plentiful witnesses anyway), Christ—now at last in a position where the High Priest could deliver Him "up to the authority and jurisdiction" of the Romans—was brought before Pilate.

The conversation between Pilate and Christ defies summary. Naturally every word of Scripture has a certain bottomlessness to it, as it is the inspired word of God. Nonetheless, the vast weight hanging upon every word spoken between these two men is almost painfully intense. John's account is certainly the most detailed and compelling. As with the question of the court of the Gentiles, the issue of where the jurisdiction of Caesar ends and the jurisdiction of the Lord begins is central to the conversation. Pilate seeks with a certain desperation to transfer the jurisdiction over Jesus back to the Sanhedrin or across to Herod Antipas but without success. At the centre of the discussion is also the question of Jesus's own

208 Mark 14:62. "And Jesus said to him: I am. And you shall see the Son of man sitting on the right hand of the power of God, and coming with the clouds of heaven."

209 Christopher Rowland, *Christian Origins: An Account of the Setting and Character of the Most Important Messianic Sect of Judaism* (London: SPCK, 1985), 165–67.

authority. Obviously, the claim to kingship is really the charge against Jesus rather than a question of jurisdiction, yet in John's account it is clear that Pilate is confusing the two issues, at least emotionally. His final action of washing his hands, unqualifiedly describing the Lord as "king of the Jews" and refusing to change the titulus when asked, implies that Pilate's final conclusion was that Christ was indeed king of the Jews and His own people had sentenced Him to death, not the governor.

The two resounding declarations "Behold the man" and "Behold your king" seem to echo the likeness and inscription to which Christ draws attention in the dialogue about the taxes; the final catastrophic declaration "we have no king but Caesar" to echo the implicit charge of idolatry with which that dialogue ends. The statement "You would have no power over me unless it had been given you from above; therefore he who delivered me to you has the greater sin" draws our attention to the different reaction Jesus exhibits to the taxes due to Caesar and the taxes due to the Temple. Neither Jesus nor Peter owes taxes to the Temple because Jesus is the Son of God and Peter is His representative. They pay by means of a miracle for the sake of avoiding scandal.[210] No such declaration is made in the case of Caesar.[211] Jesus's teaching concerning paying tax to Caesar implies that the things that are Caesar's are encompassed by, while not encompassing, the things that are God's. His statement "My kingship is not of this world; if my kingship were of this world, my servants would fight, that I might not be handed over to the Jews; but my kingship is not from the world" implies that, although obviously God has dominion over all eras and all places, there is nonetheless a sphere of influence that is at least genuinely and legitimately

[210] Matthew 17:22–27.

[211] The statement also seems to imply that, while Pilate may lawfully investigate sedition, the state *per se* has no jurisdiction in matters of revealed religion—only by delegation. This is, in fact, the traditional teaching of the Church. See Thomas Pink, "The Interpretation of *Dignitatis Humanae*: A Reply to Martin Rhonheimer," in *Nova et Vetera* 11.1 (Winter 2013): 77–121.

lent to Caesar for the duration of the age , until the new heavens and the new earth. This is certainly the implication of Boniface VIII's solemn teaching concerning the two swords.[212] The Jews on the other hand have handed over their own king, raising their hand against the Lord's anointed,[213] an act for which they have no authority. In doing so, they have transferred Him and subjected themselves "to the authority and jurisdiction" of the Romans.

There is an even more intense irony at this point, reflecting the praise of the author of 1 Maccabees for the Roman commonwealth. The Romans do not have a king; indeed, Caesar was slain on suspicion of coveting the title. Augustus took pains to eschew it. Augustus did however call himself *Divi Filius*.[214] The interplay between the two titles in the dialogue between Pilate and the Jews and Pilate and Jesus is thus laden with multiple meanings. The procurator is relaxed about the title "king" and open to either releasing or condemning the Lord depending on the "merits" of the case. It is only when he hears the title "Son of God" that he begins to fear Him.

One might suppose from reading the first few chapters of the Acts of the Apostles that the book concerns the Twelve. By the conclusion it is clear that the apostles in question are the two founders of that Church whose "faith is proclaimed in all the world,"[215] Saints Peter and Paul. From the day of Pentecost, Romans are present.[216] The dramatic hinge of the Book in chapters 9 and 10 revolves around the conversion of two Roman citizens, Saul and Cornelius, fulfilling the prophesy of Daniel 9:27 concerning the confirmation of the Covenant with the many. Finally, the book climaxes with the Lord's vessel of election—carrying His name before the Gentiles, and kings, and the children of Israel—established in Rome "preaching the

212 DH 870–75.

213 2 Samuel 1:14.

214 Syme, *Roman Revolution*, 53; 202.

215 Romans 1:8.

216 Acts 2:10.

kingdom of God, and teaching the things which concern the Lord Jesus Christ, with all confidence, without prohibition."[217]

Most of the remarks concerning obedience to the civil power in the epistles—most notably Romans 13, 1 Timothy 2:2–4 and 1 Peter 2:17—are readily understandable in terms of the de factoism of the prophets (which also seems to be implied by John 19:11). Of course, the metaphorical use of the term "sword" in Romans 13:4 helps to tie the passage into the doctrine of St Bernard and Boniface VIII.[218] In general, the assertion in verse 8, "owe no one anything, except to love one another; for he who loves his neighbour has fulfilled the law," once again implies the doctrine of the likeness and the inscription that the things that are Caesar's are encompassed by, while not encompassing, the things that are God's. The reference to Rome as Babylon in 1 Peter 5:13 seems not only to imply that St Peter is in Rome but also to suggest a more mystical significance, namely, that Rome stands as the exemplar of the earthly city in general.[219]

In some ways the most important reference in the epistles to the providential role of Rome comes in the second earliest of them, the Second Letter of St Paul to the Thessalonians, chapter two:

> Now concerning the coming of our Lord Jesus Christ and our assembling to meet him, we beg you, brethren, not to be quickly shaken in mind or excited, either by spirit or by word, or by letter purporting to be from us, to the effect that the day of the Lord has come. Let no one deceive you in any way; for that day will not come, unless the rebellion comes first, and the man of lawlessness is revealed, the son of perdition, who opposes and exalts himself against every so-called god or object of worship, so that he takes his seat in the temple of God, proclaiming himself to be God. Do you not remember that

[217] Acts 28:31.

[218] Tierney, *Crisis of Church and State*, 92–94.

[219] See St Bede, *In Primam Epistolam Petri* (PL 93:67).

> when I was still with you I told you this? And you know what is restraining him now so that he may be revealed in his time. For the mystery of lawlessness is already at work; only he who now restrains it will do so until he is out of the way. And then the lawless one will be revealed, and the Lord Jesus will slay him with the breath of his mouth and destroy him by his appearing and his coming. The coming of the lawless one by the activity of Satan will be with all power and with pretended signs and wonders, and with all wicked deception for those who are to perish, because they refused to love the truth and so be saved. Therefore God sends upon them a strong delusion, to make them believe what is false, so that all may be condemned who did not believe the truth but had pleasure in unrighteousness. But we are bound to give thanks to God always for you, brethren beloved by the Lord, because God chose you from the beginning to be saved, through sanctification by the Spirit and belief in the truth.

According to the majority of the Fathers, "what" and "he" who restrains the "lawless one" (unanimously identified by the Fathers as the Antichrist of whom John speaks in 1 John 2:18–22 and 4:3) is the Roman empire and the Roman emperor.[220] St Thomas considers in his commentary on this epistle how it could be that the Antichrist has not come by his own time when it would seem that the Roman empire has perished. "The Roman Empire has not perished," he explains, "but passed from the temporal to the spiritual order." The revolt of which St Paul speaks will be against the faith and government of the Holy Roman Church.[221]

---

[220] See below: Tertullian, St John Chrysostom, St Basil, St Cyril of Jerusalem, et al.

[221] St Thomas Aquinas: "Dicit autem Augustinus, quod hoc figuratur Dan. II, 31 in statua, ubi nominantur quatuor regna; et post illa adventus Christi, et quod hoc erat conveniens signum, quia Romanum imperium firmatum fuit ad hoc, quod sub eius potestate praedicaretur fides per totum mundum. Sed quomodo est hoc, quia iamdiu gentes recesserunt a Romano imperio, et tamen necdum venit Antichristus? Dicendum

In chapter thirty two of his *Dialogue with Trypho the Jew*, St Justin Martyr (c. 100–165) addresses the question of the "little horn" of Daniel 7:25 which will speak blasphemies against the Most High and affirms that this figure remains in the future: ". . . and he whom Daniel foretells would have dominion for a time, and times, and an half, is even already at the door, about to speak blasphemous and daring things against the Most High."[222] St Irenaeus (c. 130–202) is later than St Justin but no less powerful a witness as a pupil of St Polycarp of Smyrna, himself a disciple of St John the Evangelist. In chapter twenty-six of the fifth book of *On the Detection and Overthrow of Knowledge Falsely So Called* (usually referred to as *Adversus haereses* and written around 180), St Irenaeus identifies the figure in Daniel with a ruler arising from the ruins of the Roman empire. "In a still clearer light has John, in the Apocalypse, indicated to the Lord's disciples what shall happen in the last times, and concerning the ten kings who shall then arise, among whom the empire which now rules [the earth] shall be partitioned. He teaches us what the ten horns shall be which were seen by Daniel."[223]

In chapter thirty he clearly identifies the Antichrist of St John's first epistle with the first beast of Revelation chapter thirteen who bears the number 666 and with the "abomination of desolation of Daniel." He provides various possible meanings for this but prefers one which makes

---

est, quod nondum cessavit, sed est commutatum de temporali in spirituale, ut dicit Leo Papa in sermone de apostolis. Et ideo dicendum est, quod discessio a Romano imperio debet intelligi, non solum a temporali, sed a spirituali, scilicet a fide Catholica Romanae Ecclesiae. Est autem hoc conveniens signum, quod sicut Christus venit quando Romanum imperium omnibus dominabatur, ita e converso signum Antichristi est discessio ab eo." *Super II Thess.*, cap. 2, lec. 1.

222 PG 6:541–45. Trans. M. Dods and G. Reith, in *ANF*, vol. 1 (Buffalo, NY: Christian Literature Publishing Co., 1885), 210.

223 PG 7:1192. Trans. A. Roberts and W. Rambaut, in *ANF*, vol. 1 (Buffalo, NY: Christian Literature Publishing Co., 1885), 555.

clear the identification of the first beast of Revelation chapter thirteen with the Roman empire: "*Lateinos* has the number six hundred and sixty-six; and it is very probable, this being the name of the last kingdom. For the Latins are they who at present bear rule."[224]

In chapter twenty-four of his *On the Resurrection*, St Irenaeus's slightly younger North African contemporary Tertullian (c. 160–c. 225) is the first to make the exegesis of Thessalonians his explicit theme:

> "For the mystery of iniquity doth already work; only he who now hinders must hinder, until he be taken out of the way." What obstacle is there but the Roman state, the falling away of which, by being scattered into ten kingdoms, shall introduce Antichrist upon (its own ruins)? "And then shall be revealed the wicked one, whom the Lord shall consume with the spirit of His mouth, and shall destroy with the brightness of His coming: even him whose coming is after the working of Satan, with all power, and signs, and lying wonders, and with all deceivableness of unrighteousness in them that perish."[225]

In chapter thirty-two of his *Apology*, Tertullian explains that this teaching of St Paul secures the loyalty of the Christian to the empire—for all their refusal to express that loyalty in pagan rites:

> There is also another and a greater necessity for our offering prayer in behalf of the emperors, nay, for the complete stability of the empire, and for Roman interests in general. For we know that a mighty shock impending over the whole earth—in fact, the very end of all things threatening dreadful woes—is only retarded by the continued existence of the Roman empire. We have no desire,

[224] PG 7:1206 (ibid., 559).

[225] PL 2:829–30. Trans. P. Holmes, in *ANF*, vol. 3 (Buffalo, NY: Christian Literature Publishing Co., 1885), 563.

> then, to be overtaken by these dire events; and in praying that their coming may be delayed, we are lending our aid to Rome's duration. More than this, though we decline to swear by the genii of the Cæsars, we swear by their safety, which is worth far more than all your genii.[226]

The sainted third-century antipope St Hippolytus (170–235), whom Photios alleged to have been a pupil of St Irenaeus,[227] wrote an entire treatise *On Christ and Antichrist.* Hippolytus is illuminating in that he seems to see the prophecies of Revelation as both fulfilled and yet to come. The destruction of Babylon he sees in some sense fulfilled in that of Jerusalem—"Is not their country, Judea, desolate? Is not the holy place burned with fire?"—and yet he sees much of revelation as awaiting fulfilment and even Daniel's prophecy of the weeks[228] as relating to the second and not the first Advent of the Messiah. It is not impossible that Hippolytus believes in a double fulfilment such as we have suggested but he is not specific enough to be sure.

About many things, however, he is clear. The ten horns are ten democracies that will emerge as successor states to Rome (and these are also the ten toes of the statue in Nebuchadnezzar's dream). The eleventh horn (which is not mentioned in Revelation) is the Antichrist. The first beast of Revelation chapter thirteen is definitely Rome. Rather than seeing the second beast in that chapter as the false prophet of 16:13, 19:20, and 20:10 Hippolytus sees its two horns as symbolizing the Antichrist and the

[226] PL 1:447. Trans. S. Thelwall, in *ANF*, vol. 3 (Buffalo, NY: Christian Literature Publishing Co., 1885), 42–43.

[227] PG103:401–4. Photios, *The Library of Photius*, trans. J.H. Freese (New York: MacMillan, 1920), 211.

[228] Augustine says this is a minority opinion. St Augustine, *Letter* 199:19 to Hesychius (PL 33:904–25), in *Letters*, vol. 4, trans. W. Parsons (New York: Fathers of the Church, 1955), 370.

False Prophet separately. The worship of the beast from the sea (Rome) and of its image Hippolytus interprets as a restoration of the Augustan principate. In this way the "deadly wound" of the Roman empire will appear to have been healed. These events "signify that, after the manner of the law of Augustus, by whom the empire of Rome was established, he [the Antichrist] too will rule and govern, sanctioning everything by it, and taking greater glory to himself."[229] Thus, it would seem, the later events of chapter thirteen take place, in St Hippolytus's view, after the events of chapters fourteen to eighteen.

Once more, the implication of St Hippolytus's understanding of the end times (whether or not one accepts every detail) is that the fourth beast of Daniel is Rome and that the continuance of her empire precludes the coming of the Antichrist. Lactantius (c. 240–c. 320), Constantine the Great's advisor and the tutor to his son Crispus, concurred. In chapter twenty-five of the seventh book of his *Divinae Institutiones*, he writes:

> While the city of Rome remains it appears that nothing of this kind is to be feared. But when that capital of the world shall have fallen, and shall have begun to be a street, which the Sibyls say shall come to pass, who can doubt that the end has now arrived to the affairs of men and the whole world? It is that city, that only, which still sustains all things; and the God of heaven is to be entreated by us and implored—if, indeed, His arrangements and decrees can be delayed—lest, sooner than we think, that detestable tyrant should come.[230]

[229] PG 10:768. Trans. J.H. MacMahon, in *ANF*, vol. 5 (Buffalo, NY: Christian Literature Publishing Co., 1886), 214.

[230] PL 6:812–13. Trans. W. Fletcher, in *ANF*, vol. 7 (Buffalo, NY: Christian Literature Publishing Co., 1886), 220. "Illa, illa est civitas, quae adhuc sustentat omnia; precandusque nobis et adorandus est Deus coeli; si tamen statuta eius et placita differi possunt, ne citius quam putemus tyrannus ille abominabilis veniat."

As was observed by Tertullian, this doctrine is most helpful in establishing the loyalty of the Christian faithful to the Roman empire, and it could hardly be expected to perish in the face of Constantine's universal triumph of 324.[231] In fact, the patristic doctrine is neatly summarized by St Cyril of Jerusalem (c. 315–386) in his fifteenth Catechetical Lecture:

> But this aforesaid Antichrist is to come when the times of the Roman empire shall have been fulfilled, and the end of the world is now drawing near. There shall rise up together ten kings of the Romans, reigning in different parts perhaps, but all about the same time; and after these an eleventh, the Antichrist, who by his magical craft shall seize upon the Roman power; and of the kings who reigned before him, three he shall humble, and the remaining seven he shall keep in subjection to himself. At first indeed he will put on a show of mildness (as though he were a learned and discreet person), and of soberness and benevolence: and by the lying signs and wonders of his magical deceit and having beguiled the Jews, as though he were the expected Christ, he shall afterwards be characterized by all kinds of crimes of inhumanity and lawlessness, so as

[231] Gregory the Great (or rather St Benedict) did not hold that the Fall of Rome in 410 or its tribulations in the centuries that followed constituted the destruction which is prerequisite to the coming of the end. "It may be farther observed that holy men in the early Church certainly thought that the barbarian invasions were not all that Rome was to receive in the way of vengeance, but that God would one day destroy it by the fury of the elements. 'Rome,' says Pope Gregory, at a time when a barbarian conqueror had possession of the city, and all things seemed to threaten its destruction, 'Rome shall not be destroyed by the nations, but shall consume away internally, worn out by storms of lightning, whirlwinds, and earthquakes.' In accordance with this is the prophecy ascribed to St. Malachy of Armagh, a mediæval archbishop (AD 1130), which declares, 'In the last persecution of the Holy Church, Peter of Rome shall be on the throne, who shall feed his flock in many tribulations. When these are past, the city upon seven hills shall be destroyed, and the awful Judge shall judge the people.'" St John Henry Newman, "Advent Sermons on Antichrist," in *Discussions and Arguments*, 86–87.

> to outdo all unrighteous and ungodly men who have gone before him, displaying against all men, but especially against us Christians, a spirit murderous and most cruel, merciless and crafty. And after perpetrating such things for three years and six months only, he shall be destroyed by the glorious second advent from heaven of the only-begotten Son of God, our Lord and Saviour Jesus, the true Christ, who shall slay Antichrist with the breath of His mouth, and shall deliver him over to the fire of hell.[232]

A little under a century after the acclamation of Constantine, in his fourth homily on Second Thessalonians St John Chrysostom (c. 347–407) once again considers the question of the one who restrains. It seems that by this point alternative interpretations had been considered, but St John sticks with the traditional exegesis:

> "And now ye know that which restraineth, to the end that he may be revealed in his own season. For the mystery of lawlessness doth already work: only there is one that restraineth now, until he be taken out of the way. And then shall be revealed the lawless one, whom the Lord Jesus shall slay with the breath of His mouth, and bring to nought by the manifestation of His coming: even he whose coming is according to the working of Satan."
>
> One may naturally enquire, what is that which withholdeth, and after that would know, why Paul expresses it so obscurely. What then is it that withholdeth, that is, hindereth him from being revealed? Some indeed say, the grace of the Spirit, but others the Roman empire, to whom I most of all accede. Wherefore? Because if he meant to say the Spirit, he would not have spoken obscurely, but plainly, that even now the grace of the Spirit, that is the gifts,

[232] PG 33:885. Trans. E. H. Gifford, in *NPNF* II, vol. 7 (Buffalo, NY: Christian Literature Publishing Co., 1894), 107–8.

withhold him. And otherwise he ought now to have come, if he was about to come when the gifts ceased; for they have long since ceased. But because he said this of the Roman empire, he naturally glanced at it, and speaks covertly and darkly. For he did not wish to bring upon himself superfluous enmities, and useless dangers. . . . And he did not say that it will be quickly, although he is always saying it—but what? "that he may be revealed in his own season," he says, "For the mystery of lawlessness doth already work." He speaks here of Nero, as if he were the type of Antichrist. For he too wished to be thought a god. And he has well said, "the mystery"; that is, it worketh not openly, as the other, nor without shame. For if there was found a man before that time, he means, who was not much behind Antichrist in wickedness, what wonder, if there shall now be one? But he did not also wish to point him out plainly: and this not from cowardice, but instructing us not to bring upon ourselves unnecessary enmities, when there is nothing to call for it. So indeed he also says here. "Only there is one that restraineth now, until he be taken out of the way," that is, when the Roman empire is taken out of the way, then he shall come. And naturally. For as long as the fear of this empire lasts, no one will willingly exalt himself, but when that is dissolved, he will attack the anarchy, and endeavour to seize upon the government both of man and of God. For as the kingdoms before this were destroyed, for example, that of the Medes by the Babylonians, that of the Babylonians by the Persians, that of the Persians by the Macedonians, that of the Macedonians by the Romans: so will this also be by the Antichrist, and he by Christ, and it will no longer withhold. And these things Daniel delivered to us with great clearness.

"And then," he says, "shall be revealed the lawless one." And what after this? The consolation is at hand. "Whom the Lord Jesus shall slay with the breath of His mouth, and bring to nought by the

> manifestation of His coming, even he whose coming is according to the working of Satan."[233]

The testimony of St Cyril and St John Chrysostom is significant as the evidence surviving up to the fourth century—Irenaeus, Hippolytus, Justin—is entirely western albeit originating from the east. The Latin Doctors of the fourth and fifth century remain consistent with their predecessors. St Ambrose (c. 340—397) asserts:

> The Lord will not return until the Roman rule fails and antichrist appears, who will kill the saints, giving back freedom to the Romans but under his own name.[234]

St Jerome (c. 340–420) in his Commentary on Daniel 7:8 confirms:

> We should therefore concur with the traditional interpretation of all the commentators of the Christian Church, that at the end of the world, when the Roman Empire is to be destroyed, there shall be ten kings who will partition the Roman world amongst themselves. Then an insignificant eleventh king will arise, who will overcome three of the ten kings.[235]

Likewise, in his *De Civitate Dei* St Augustine (345–430) expounds St Paul in the same sense, although with a little more reservation:

> For what does he mean by "For the mystery of iniquity doth already work: only he who now holdeth, let him hold until he be taken

[233] PG 62:485. Trans. J. A. Broadus, in *NPNF* I, vol. 13 (Buffalo, NY: Christian Literature Publishing Co., 1889), 388–89.

[234] Ambrose on II Thess. (PL 17:481).

[235] Jerome, *Commentary on Daniel*, 7.6 (PL 25:667), trans. G.L. Archer (Eugene, OR: Wipf & Stock, 2009), 77. See also *Jerome's Commentary on Daniel: A Study of Comparative Jewish and Christian Interpretations of the Hebrew Bible*, trans. J. Braverman (Washington, DC: Catholic Biblical Association of America, 1978), 77.

> out of the way: and then shall the wicked be revealed"? I frankly confess I do not know what he means. . . . However, it is not absurd to believe that these words of the apostle, "Only he who now holdeth, let him hold until he be taken out of the way," refer to the Roman empire, as if it were said, "Only he who now reigneth, let him reign until he be taken out of the way." "And then shall the wicked be revealed": no one doubts that this means Antichrist.[236]

The Book of Revelation is, naturally, an enigma and is all the less decipherable because a great deal of it may well refer to events that have not yet transpired or are not even near to us in time. It also quite obviously has a great deal to say about Rome, most of it negative. Even were one to take an exclusively futurist interpretation of the text, it is clear that, at the very least, Rome plays a huge typological role. In fact, despite the plausibility and popularity of preterism or seeing the prophecies as pertaining to the past among contemporary orthodox Catholics (i.e., those professing *inter alia* the unlimited material inerrancy of Scripture),[237] an entirely preterist interpretation of the literal sense of Revelation is excluded by the prohibition of Trent and Vatican I against the reading of Scripture contrary to the unanimous interpretation of the Fathers.[238]

It appears that (with, as we shall see, the possible exception of Eusebius of Caesarea) the first author to present a comprehensive preterist interpretation of Revelation was Luis del Alcázar S.J. (1554–1613) in his 1614 *Vestigatio arcani sensus in Apocalypsi*, published posthumously.[239] The

[236] Augustine, *City of God*, 20, 19, trans. M. Dods, in *NPNF* I, vol. 2 (Buffalo, NY: Christian Literature Publishing Co., 1887), 437–38.

[237] Michael Patrick Barber, *Coming Soon: Unlocking the Book of Revelation and Applying Its Lessons Today* (Steubenville, OH: Emmaus Road, 2005).

[238] DH 1507; 1863; 3007.

[239] Judith Kovacs and Christopher Rowland, *Revelation: The Apocalypse of Jesus Christ* (Oxford: Blackwell, 2004), 11. See Thomas Hobbes's succinct and hostile epitome of this thesis: "The Papacy is not other than the Ghost of the deceased Roman Empire,

attraction for a Spanish Jesuit of the Counter-Reformation in an interpretation of Revelation as having been largely fulfilled in the past lies in the ease with which Protestant commentators were able to interpret the text as an indictment of the supposed spiritual tyranny of the papacy.[240]

The allegation of novelty must be qualified, however, as St Augustine[241] and others (though not Saints Papias or Irenaeus) firmly placed the millennium of chapter 19 in the present, though they did not abandon the application of the earlier parts of the text to the future. This may already indicate the potential reconciliation of preterist, historicist, and futurist readings of the text. As has been pointed out, Matthew 5:17–18 implies that the Crucifixion, the fall of the Temple in AD 70, and the end of the present world are all in some sense the same event. Consequently, an exhaustively preterist reading of the last book of Scripture need not, necessarily, be an exclusively preterist reading.

It is quite clear that the identity of the fourth beast in Daniel is of tremendous importance to the interpretation of the Apocalypse as both the Dragon of Revelation 12 and the first Beast of Revelation 13 are given its key characteristic: ten horns. Both the Dragon and the Beast also have seven heads and, in fact, Revelation 17:9 even tells us outright that "the seven heads are [among other things] seven mountains." If St John did not intend the connection to Rome to be drawn, then he must at least have expected it. The first beast of Revelation 13, the "beast rising out of the sea," is composed of elements from all four of the beasts of Daniel 7: "I saw a beast rising out of the sea, with ten horns and seven heads, with ten diadems upon its horns and a blasphemous name upon its heads and the beast that I saw was like a leopard, its feet were like a bear's, and its mouth

---

sitting crowned upon the grave thereof." *Leviathan* (Oxford: Oxford World's Classics, 2008), 463.

240 Nevertheless a key text in the recent revival of interest in preterism is a Protestant work: David Chilton, *The Days of Vengeance* (Ft. Worth, TX: Dominion Press, 1987).

241 *City of God* 20, 7.

was like a lion's mouth." As Daniel tells us comparatively little about the appearance of the fourth beast, it is hard to tell if the beast from the sea is intended to be a composite of all four or to be the fourth. We shall assume that, from a preterist perspective at least, it is the fourth beast.[242]

The seven horns of the beast from the sea in the Apocalypse receive extensive interpretation in the text itself. They are "seven kings"[243] and "seven hills."[244] The heads bear "names of blasphemy."[245] The sixth receives a mortal wound and yet recovers.[246] The recovery of the beast wins it the adulation of the "whole earth" (ὅλη ἡ γῆ).[247] Obviously the meaning of the earth/land is crucial here. It might be taken to mean the entire world, but this hardly does justice to the contrast with the sea. Following the preterist path where it leads us, it is hard to resist the interpretation that the earth denotes Israel and the sea denotes the Gentiles.[248] The six horns prior to the one which reigns but briefly would then be the first six of Suetonius's twelve Caesars. Yet in what sense could the Jews be said to have worshiped Nero? This is a red herring. It is Nero who receives the wound, but the beast is pagan Rome. It is the empire which is worshiped. No less a figure than Josephus himself tells us in a matter of fact sort of way that Vespasian is the Messiah.[249]

The key questions in regard to Rome and Revelation are the identity of the beast from the sea, the beast from the land, and the whore of Babylon. Contemporary preterism identifies these as the Roman empire, the Jewish opponents of the Gospel, and the Jerusalem establishment respectively.[250]

---

[242] Although it might be equally legitimate to say that the fourth beast is the temporal power in general when unsubjected to the spiritual.

[243] Revelation 17:10.

[244] Revelation 17:9.

[245] Revelation 13:1.

[246] Revelation 13:3.

[247] Ibid.

[248] Especially as Daniel 7:3 describes all four beasts as coming out of the sea.

[249] *Jewish War* 6.312–13.

[250] Chilton, *Days of Vengeance*, 135–45; Barber, *Coming Soon*, 175.

The two heavenly witnesses of chapter eleven provide a particular challenge and so their correct identification may pay special dividends. These are opposed and martyred by the Beast which ascends from the abyss[251] who is here introduced without explanation, despite the fact that it will be introduced as if for the first time in chapter thirteen.[252] This reinforces the impression that the same events are being recounted from various perspectives throughout the book, as does the fourfold repetition of the period of three and a half years in this and the two succeeding chapters (11:2; 11:3; 12:6; 13:5). This is the length of time of the persecutions prophesied in Daniel and of the prophesy of Elijah prior to the confrontation on Mount Carmel.[253]

One possible explanation would be that the two witnesses are Moses and Elijah,[254] literally at the end of time and figuratively prior to the destruction of the Temple. That is to say, in a figurative sense, the Law and the Prophets witness against unbelieving Israel,[255] their testimony is rejected, and they become the exclusive property of the New Israel, i.e., ascend into heaven.[256] The earthquake in which seven thousand men die and a tenth of the city is destroyed[257] would seem to indicate that there are no more righteous men practicing the ritual law of the Old Covenant, for this is the number of those who did not bend the knee to Baal in Elijah's time, a number invoked by Paul in regard to the remnant of righteous Jews in his own day.[258] The

---

[251] Revelation 11:7.

[252] Revelation 13:1.

[253] Daniel 7:25; 12:7; 1 Kings 17–18; Chilton, *Day of Vengeance*, 116.

[254] An identification most obviously suggested by the powers attributed to the two witnesses, their appearance at the Transfiguration, and the implication in Jude 1:9 that Moses was miraculously resuscitated and assumed. Dom Bernard Orchard, et al., *A Catholic Commentary on Holy Scripture* (London: Thomas Nelson & Sons, 1953), 1201.

[255] Luke 16:29–31.

[256] Revelation 11:12.

[257] Also an OT symbolic proportion of the remnant: Amos 5:3; Isaiah 6:13. See Richard Bauckham, *The Climax of Prophecy* (London: T&T Clark, 1993), 282.

[258] 1 Kings 19:18; Romans 11:4.

Israel referred to in 1 Kings is the northern kingdom of the ten tribes. It is noticeable that the tribe of Dan is excluded from the list of tribes from which one hundred and forty-four thousand are sealed in chapter seven; why this is is unclear, but that would constitute one tenth of Israel. Christ is clear in John chapter four that the Samaritans err concerning the true cult of God, but He is equally clear that the matter will very soon be of only academic interest. By the time St John transcribed his vision, all the adherents of the Old Law had become in this sense Samaritans.

It is also not impossible that the two heavenly witnesses are St Peter and St Paul. This would be especially convincing if we took the two witnesses to be Enoch and Elijah (the majority opinion among the fathers)[259] as these are described in Ecclesiasticus 48:10 and Ecclesiasticus 44:16, namely, as charged with the conversion of the Gentiles and the Jews respectively, which is of course the missionary division between Ss Peter and Paul according to Galatians 2:7.[260] This process by which the residual presence of the old ritual law passes away would be quasi-automatic, as the Council of Florence defines[261] that from the death of Christ the Old Law ceased to justify. One may assume that those already justified by faith in the coming Messiah who were invincibly ignorant of His arrival did not suddenly fall into mortal sin at 3pm on Good Friday, but should they so fall subsequently, no act of faith made through the Old Law would save them nor would anyone be cleansed of original sin by that means thereafter.[262] This period from the crucifixion to the martyrdoms of Peter and Paul would also be the length of time it took for all the Israelites who left

[259] Orchard, *Catholic Commentary*, 1201.

[260] This might still work with Moses and Elijah if we supposed the Law to be the business of the Jews alone while prophecy concerns the Messianic universal mission.

[261] DH 1348.

[262] St Thomas Aquinas, *De Veritate*, Q. 14, art. 12.

Egypt to die in the desert.[263] The association of those Jews who observe the Law but reject the Messiah with the northern kingdom of Israel also fits with the references at Revelation 2:9 and 3:9 to those "who say that they are Jews and are not."

If the beast of chapter eleven is the first beast of chapter thirteen (and "the sea" seems closer to "the abyss" than "the land"), then we have the Roman empire slaying Saints Peter and Paul at the instigation of the unbelieving Jews during the Neronian persecution (AD 64–67 = 11:2, 11:3, 13:5) of three and a half years as the final expression of their rejection of the Law and the Prophets whom the two apostles embody. This rejection is then followed by the three and a half year period (AD 66–70 = 12:6) from the outbreak of the First Jewish War to the destruction of the Temple.

Once the utility of the Old Law is extinguished, the manifestation of the Church in her glory is completed, the sanctuary of God in heaven opens, and the Ark of the Covenant, the Woman clothed with the Sun, is revealed. By the same logic, the enemy of the Church, the terrible red Dragon, is forced to show his hand. But the enemy cannot destroy the Messiah or his brethren or the Church which flees into the desert for three and a half years, just as the faithful fled Jerusalem for Pella. "But the people of the church in Jerusalem had been commanded by a revelation, vouchsafed to approved men there before the war, to leave the city and to dwell in a certain town of Perea called Pella."[264]

There are many parallels and direct quotations from Zechariah chapter four in Revelation chapter eleven. It is in Zechariah where the two witnesses first appear as a motif. In Zechariah 4:2–3 they are two olive trees on either side of a single menorah. In Revelation 11:4 they are "the two olive trees and the two lampstands which stand before the Lord of

[263] Deuteronomy 2:14.

[264] Eusebius, *History of the Church* 3.5.3.

the earth." If the intuition about Peter and Paul and their respective missions is correct, then this divergence may have a simple explanation. When Zechariah had his vision there was one authorized cult (the Old Law), but both the Jews themselves and the God-fearing Gentiles could be justified through this covenant. Hence, two olive trees but one menorah. In Revelation 11, prior to the fall of the Temple but after the death of Christ there are two cults which are acceptable means of worship to God: the ritual law of the Old and New Testaments,[265] hence two olive trees and two menorahs. In Romans 11, however, we discover that a process of pruning and engrafting, gathering into one the scattered children of God, is occurring by which there will soon be only one olive tree. As St Bede teaches, "the lampstand in the tabernacle represents the church universal of the present time."[266] Andrew of Caesarea provides a compelling answer for the meaning of the seven lampstands. St John himself tells us that the seven churches are the seven lampstands.[267] According to Andrew the seven churches of Revelation represent the church universal.[268] Furthermore, he tells us that some held that the lampstand of Ephesus was removed (as threatened) in 451 when the patriarchate of Constantinople was created. "Some understood the removal of the lampstand to refer to the removal of the archpriest of Ephesus, because it was moved to the seat of the King [*Basileus*]."[269] It is not unreasonable therefore to see in

[265] Strictly speaking, the Old Law died on the Cross; although not yet deadly, it cannot be put on the same level of acceptability as the New Law. It would be more accurate to say that the two candlesticks represent the Church as gathered from the Jews (for whom at that time the use of old ritual remained licit) and the Gentiles (for whom it did not).

[266] St Bede, *On the Tabernacle*, trans. A.G. Holder (Liverpool: Liverpool University Press, 1994), 31.

[267] Revelation 1:20.

[268] Andrew of Caesarea, *Commentary on the Apocalypse*, trans. E.S. Constantinou (Washington, DC: Catholic University of America Press, 2011), 56.

[269] Andrew of Caesarea, *Commentary on the Apocalypse*, 64.

the seven lampstands of Revelation[270] an expression of the constitutive character of the seven ritual churches within the Catholic Church.[271]

Three times in Revelation (2:27, 12:5, 19:15) the prophecy of Psalm 2:9 is invoked: "Ask of me, and I will make the nations your heritage, and the ends of the earth your possession. You shall break them with a rod of iron, and dash them in pieces like a potter's vessel." On the second two occasions it relates directly to the Messiah's rule over the nations. On the first occasion it relates to the participation of Christians in this government. This prophesy of the Psalms has special resonance as here we have the two materials from which the bottom of Nebuchadnezzar's statue is built, a statue which is indeed broken in pieces by the smashing of its feet of clay. Andrew of Caesarea in his seventh-century commentary has illuminating observations on this point, drawing together the first and second passages.

> Continuously the Church gives birth to Christ through those who are baptized, as if he is being fashioned in them until the completion of their spiritual age, according to the Apostle. A male child is the people of the Church who are not feminized by pleasures, through whom Christ God shepherded the nations, even already by the powerful iron-like hands of the strong Romans.[272]

---

[270] If the seven lampstands are churches, so must be the two lampstands (the church of the Jews and the church of the Gentiles). It might be also that, if the seven lampstands are representative of the whole church, since seven is the number of completeness, the two lampstands stand for the church in its role *as witness*, according to the well-known Biblical requirement that evidence be accepted only on the testimony of two witnesses. One is reminded of the pairing of Sibyls and Prophets in the Sistine chapel.

[271] J.N.D. Kelly, *Golden Mouth: The Story of John Chrysostom—Ascetic, Preacher, Bishop* (Ithaca, NY: Cornell University Press, 1995), 174. "Although not a patriarchal see (and never to become one), Ephesos was a leading ecclesiastical centre, and seems to have claimed some sort of primacy over the provinces adjacent to Asia itself . . . the entire civil diocese of Asiana."

[272] Andrew of Caesarea, *Commentary on the Apocalypse*, 140.

Back in the fourth century, Cyril of Jerusalem read Psalm 2 in the same sense.

> But again you ask yet another testimony of the time. "The Lord said to Me, You are My Son; this day have I begotten You": and a few words further on, "You shall rule them with a rod of iron." I have said before that the kingdom of the Romans is clearly called a rod of iron; but what is wanting concerning this let us further call to mind out of Daniel. For in relating and interpreting to Nebuchadnezzar the image of the statue, he tells also his whole vision concerning it: and that a stone cut out of a mountain without hands, that is, not set up by human contrivance, should overpower the whole world: and he speaks most clearly thus; "And in the days of those kingdoms the God of heaven shall set up a kingdom, which shall never be destroyed, and His kingdom shall not be left to another people" (Daniel 2:44).[273]

The armies of Titus arrived at the walls of Jerusalem on the Day of Passover AD 70, forty years to the day after the Crucifixion of the Messiah.[274] In virtue of the Neronian persecution and the First Jewish War, the translation of covenant from the Jews to the Romans is completed: "Then the seventh angel blew his trumpet, and there were loud voices in heaven, saying, 'The kingdom of the world has become the kingdom of our Lord and of his Christ, and he shall reign for ever and ever.'"[275]

---

[273] PG 33:748. Trans. E. H. Gifford, in *NPNF* II, vol. 7 (Buffalo, NY: Christian Literature Publishing Co., 1894), 76–77. See also the mysterious remark in Book 5 of St Aphrahat's *Demonstrations*: "At His coming He handed over the kingdom to the Romans, as the children of Esau are called. And these children of Esau will keep the kingdom for its giver." Trans. J. Gwynn, in *NPNF* II, vol. 13 (Buffalo, NY: Christian Literature Publishing Co., 1890), 358.

[274] Benedict XVI, *Jesus of Nazareth. Holy Week: From the Entrance into Jerusalem to the Resurrection*, Part 2 (San Francisco: Ignatius Press, 2011), 30.

[275] Revelation 11:15.

It seems reasonable to suppose that the vision occurring in chapter twelve after the sanctuary of God in heaven is opened *is* the secret contained in the scroll and proclaimed by the trumpets whose earthly realization is then described in the succeeding chapters. Certainly, this chapter provides the hinge of the book.

The Dragon, Satan, gives his authority to the Beast from the sea that is the Roman empire, as he boasted he could.[276] There are seven heads for the seven Caesars who reigned up to the time of the First Jewish War, ten horns for the ten barbarian successor kingdoms, the toes of its feet of clay.[277] This beast combines the characteristics and the power of the first three beasts of Daniel's prophecy—not an unfitting description of that empire which was able uniquely to encompass Western civilization and to rule one quarter of mankind for five hundred years (c. 50 BC to AD 450). Indeed, as St John Henry Newman would have it (commenting on 2 Thessalonians), it endured into his own day:

> It is not clear that the Roman Empire is gone. Far from it: the Roman Empire in the view of prophecy, remains even to this day. Rome had a very different fate from the other three monsters mentioned by the Prophet, as will be seen by his description of it. "Behold a fourth beast, dreadful and terrible, and strong exceedingly; and it had great iron teeth: it devoured and brake in pieces, and stamped the residue with the feet of it: and it was diverse from all the beasts that were before it, and it had ten horns." [Dan. vii. 7.] These ten horns, an Angel informed him, "are ten kings that shall rise out of this kingdom" of Rome. As, then, the ten horns belonged to the fourth beast, and were not separate from it, so the kingdoms, into which the Roman Empire was to be divided, are but the continuation

[276] Matthew 4:8–9; Luke 4:5–7.

[277] Chilton, *Days of Vengeance*, 136.

and termination of that Empire itself,—which lasts on, and in some sense lives in the view of prophecy, however we decide the historical question. Consequently, we have not yet seen the end of the Roman Empire. "That which withholdeth" still exists, up to the manifestation of its ten horns; and till it is removed, Antichrist will not come. And from the midst of those horns he will arise, as the same Prophet informs us: "I considered the horns, and behold, there came up among them another little horn; . . . and behold, in this horn were eyes like the eyes of a man, and a mouth speaking great things."[278]

Remarkably, at least from a modern perspective, this idea that the barbarian kingdoms were an extension of the Roman dominion was even the understanding of the barbarians themselves. As Theodoric the Ostrogothic king of Italy (or rather his amanuensis Cassiodorus) wrote to the Eastern emperor, "our empire is an imitation of yours . . . a copy of the only empire on earth."[279] The first Catholic barbarian king, Clovis, received the Consular office from the emperor Anastasius (491–518) as the climax of his success, and St Ethelbert of Kent, the first Christian English king, promulgated laws "based on Roman exemplars."[280] In the same way, the Slav kingdoms which progressively absorbed more and more of the Eastern empire as she was weakened by the advance of Islam sought to obtain for themselves titles ecclesiastical and civil from the emperor in Constantinople—concessions that nevertheless implied some sort of ultimate suzerainty for the Roman ruler, binding them into the so-called

278 Newman, "Patristical Idea of Antichrist," 50–51.

279 Boethius, *The Consolation of Philosophy*, trans. V.E. Watts (London: Penguin, 2003), xix.

280 ". . . decreta illi iudiciorum iuxta exempla Romanorum." In Patrick Wormald, *The Making of English Law: King Alfred to the Twelfth Century* (Oxford: Blackwell Publishers, 1999), 29. Bede, *Historical Works: Ecclesiastical History of the English Nation: Based on the Version of Thomas Stapleton (1565)*, vol. 1 (Cambridge, MA: Harvard University Press, 1999), 226.

"Byzantine Commonwealth."[281] The states of the modern West descend from these sub-Roman polities.

The little horn, the Antichrist of the end times, has yet to come. But the wounded head is Nero. It is not the head *per se* which survives the wound, it is the Beast. And the Beast persecuted the Church for three and half years. Those who dwell in the land worship the Beast. They declared they had no king but Caesar, they procured the persecution of Nero through Poppaea,[282] and in the person of "Flavius" Josephus they acclaimed him Messiah when he had destroyed the Temple. But more than the Roman empire in particular, the Beast is the City of the World: the brigandage of violence and earthly power. The idolatrous worship of the Beast expresses the will to use the things that are God's to purchase the things that are Caesar's, and vice versa; to make grace purchasable and quantifiable, as the Samaritan Simon Magus sought to do.[283] The parallelism between the authority of the Beast from the Sea and the Messiah is emphasized by the very similar language of 13:7 and 5:9, 7:9, 11:9 and 14:6, and by the echo of St Michael's name in the blasphemous adulation of 13:4. This moral sense is confirmed by 13:10's echo of Christ's rebuke to Peter in Matthew 26:52. As He says to Pilate: "my kingdom is not of this world; if my kingdom

281 Dimitri Obolensky, *The Byzantine Commonwealth: Eastern Europe, 500–1453* (London: Sphere Books, 1974).

282 Who Josephus implies was a Jewish proselyte: *Antiquities* 20.8.11.

283 Acts 8:15–24. Simon Magus is seen as a model for the Antichrist by Bede: "In imitation of our true Head, Antichrist, who belongs to the heads of the earthly kingdom, dares to present himself as having risen from the dead, in order that he might be taken for Christ, who really did this. The fallacy of this fabrication is said to have been foreshadowed in Simon Magus." *Commentary on Revelation*, trans. F. Wallis (Liverpool: Liverpool University Press, 2013), 198. It seems highly likely that the figures of Simon Magus and Poppaea in some way lie behind the Beast from the Land and the Whore of Babylon. The matter is confused by the divergent traditions that have come down to us as to the particular role played by these two individuals in regard to Saints Peter and Paul and the Roman Church.

were of this world, my servants would fight, that I might not be handed over to the Jews; but my kingship is not from the world."[284]

Who then is the second Beast (cf. Revelation 13:11)? He arises from the land, from the people of Israel. He has two horns like a lamb but he speaks with the voice of the Dragon. This is clearly the great religious deception of the Antichrist which will come definitively at the end but is present already in the apostolic age, as John himself observed: "Children, it is the last hour; and as you have heard that antichrist is coming, so now many antichrists have come; therefore we know that it is the last hour."[285] The *Catechism* explains:

> Before Christ's second coming the Church must pass through a final trial that will shake the faith of many believers. The persecution that accompanies her pilgrimage on earth will unveil the "mystery of iniquity" in the form of a religious deception offering men an apparent solution to their problems at the price of apostasy from the truth. The supreme religious deception is that of the Antichrist, a pseudo-messianism by which man glorifies himself in place of God and of his Messiah come in the flesh. The Antichrist's deception already begins to take shape in the world every time the claim is made to realize within history that messianic hope which can only be realized beyond history through the eschatological judgment. The Church has rejected even modified forms of this falsification of the kingdom to come under the name of millenarianism, especially the "intrinsically perverse" political form of a secular messianism. The Church will enter the glory of the kingdom only through this final Passover, when she will follow her Lord in his death and Resurrection. The kingdom will be fulfilled, then, not by a historic triumph of the Church through a progressive ascendancy, but only

[284] John 18:36.

[285] 1 John 2:18.

> by God's victory over the final unleashing of evil, which will cause his Bride to come down from heaven. God's triumph over the revolt of evil will take the form of the Last Judgment after the final cosmic upheaval of this passing world.[286]

It would seem from this that (as with Hippolytus) the term Antichrist can be applied to either beast: the temporal ruler and his realm or the religious force and the false teacher. The latter would have us worship the temporal ruler and a state enslaved to the Evil One, which exercises the power of that state as it does the power of the Prince of this World:[287]

> Every institution is inspired, at least implicitly, by a vision of man and his destiny, from which it derives the point of reference for its judgment, its hierarchy of values, its line of conduct. Most societies have formed their institutions in the recognition of a certain pre-eminence of man over things. Only the divinely revealed religion has clearly recognized man's origin and destiny in God, the Creator and Redeemer. The Church invites political authorities to measure their judgments and decisions against this inspired truth about God and man: "Societies not recognizing this vision or rejecting it in the name of their independence from God are brought to seek their criteria and goal in themselves or to borrow them from some ideology. Since they do not admit that one can defend an objective criterion of good and evil, they arrogate to themselves an explicit or implicit totalitarian power over man and his destiny, as history shows."[288]

Here the anomaly of St Thomas's praise for the Augustan mode of government and St Hippolytus's prediction that this will be the mode of government of the Antichrist resolves itself. It is not an inferior and

[286] CCC 675–77.

[287] Revelation 13:2 and 12.

[288] CCC 2244, citing John Paul II, *Centesimus Annus* 45–46.

defective civil order whose natural goodness will be used to deceive the nations. The worst is the corruption of the best. From the preterist perspective however, the relationship between the two beasts must differ from the relationship between the first Beast and the Whore. The second beast, now called the false prophet, remains with the first beast until they are both cast into the lake of fire (Rev 19:20). The second beast is the spirit of heresy, which always ends up directing man's worship to the state. The Whore is specifically that conspiracy of apostate Israel in all its forms, Herodians, Sadducees, and Pharisees with the Roman power (founded upon the lust for temporal goods and the belief that the gift of God might be purchased), which is destroyed when the Roman Beast turns upon and devours the Whore. The Zealots are only the exception which proves the rule, for their rebellion against the Romans is inspired by the same temporal distortion of the Covenant as inspired the others to compromise.

In Matthew 16 and Mark 8, two accounts are given of what is clearly the same incident. In Matthew Jesus cautions the disciples against the yeast of the Pharisees and Sadducees, and in Mark against the yeast of the Pharisees and the yeast of Herod. The meaning of this saying (which mystifies the disciples) is, the Lord indicates, connected to the different number of baskets of scraps left over from the two miracles of feeding: twelve from the five thousand and seven from the four thousand. As we have seen, the death of Christ, the destruction of the Temple, and the end of the world are in some sense the same event. The twelve baskets would seem to point to the destruction of the Temple and the ensuing new people of God, while the seven baskets point to the end of the world and the new heaven and new earth. Leaven of course is what makes participation in the Passover, in Christ's death, impossible. Matthew tells us that the leaven is the teaching of the Pharisees and the Sadducees. Luke tells us that the yeast of the Pharisees is hypocrisy.[289] Whatever the yeast of the Sadducees is, it would seem to be the same error

[289] Luke 12:1.

as the yeast of Herod. They have little in common except a willingness to sacrifice spiritual for temporal goods. As Caiaphas declares, "it is better for one man to die for the people." The hypocrisy of the Pharisees prevents us from participating in Christ's death, that is, it is incompatible with justifying faith. The sacrilege of Herod and the Sadducees prevents us from sharing in the resurrection: it kills charity in the soul. The Pharisees in their hypocrisy think they can fulfil the law. They offer created goods in barter for uncreated. The Sadducees and Herod seek to procure created goods in barter for uncreated. Once more we return to the money changers in the Temple. We must render to Caesar what is his and to God what is His. We may not render what is Caesar's to God in exchange for what is His gift nor may we render God's gift to Caesar in exchange for what is his. This is why Simon Magus is the type of the false prophet who would have us worship Nero Caesar. In the light of these considerations, the chief priests' unwillingness to enter the Antonia Fortress because it was unpurged of yeast (John 16:28) is another terrifying instance of divine irony.[290]

This insight, of the essential connection[291] between the sin of the money changers (and of the priesthood in exploiting their services) and the first heresy of Simon Magus, is emphasised by St Gregory the Great in his sermon on Matthew 10:5–8.

> "You have received freely, give freely." He foresaw that some, having received this gift of the Spirit, would turn it into business use, and would debase the miraculous signs, yielding to avarice. Thus Simon the magician, being very eager to produce miracles by the imposition of hands, wished to receive the gift of the Holy Spirit for money. He could then commit a greater sin by selling what he

[290] See van Bruggen, *Christ on Earth*.

[291] St Thomas concurs: "By the dove is understood the Holy Spirit; hence those selling doves are the prelates selling spiritual gifts." *Commentary on the Gospel of Matthew, Chapters 13–28* (Lander, WY: Aquinas Institute, 2013), 213.

had purchased through wickedness. Thus too, our Redeemer made a scourge of cords, and drove the crowds from the temple, and overturned the seats of those who were selling doves which means to grant the imposition of hands, by which the Spirit is received, not for the merit of the recipient's life, but for a price.[292]

Pope Paschal I (817–825), as recorded in Gratian's Decretals, goes so far as to decree that "manifest simoniacs should be rejected by the faithful as the first and preeminent heretics; and if after admonition they refuse to desist, they should be suppressed by the secular power. For all other sins in comparison with the heresy of simony are as if of no account."[293] In Letter 146, St Peter Damian calls it "the heresy of simony, the first of all heresies to spring from the bowels of the devil."[294]

[292] PL 76:1091. *Gregory the Great: Forty Gospel Homilies*, trans. H.D. Gregory (Kalamazoo, MI: Cistercian Publications, 1990), 123. The attempt to establish a proportion between the natural and supernatural is not only the essence of Simony, the first heresy, and of Gnosticism, its child, but also of Modernism, "the synthesis of all heresies" (Pius X, *Pascendi Dominici Gregis* §39). In *Pascendi* §37 we read: "We cannot but deplore once more, and grievously, that there are Catholics who, while rejecting immanence as a doctrine, employ it as a method of apologetics, and who do this so imprudently that they seem to admit that there is in human nature a true and rigorous necessity with regard to the supernatural order—and not merely a capacity and a suitability for the supernatural order, such as has at all times been emphasized by Catholic apologists. Truth to tell it is only the moderate Modernists who make this appeal to an exigency for the Catholic religion. As for the others, who might be called integralists, they would show to the non-believer, hidden away in the very depths of his being, the very germ which Christ Himself bore in His conscience, and which He bequeathed to the world." Cf. Pius XII in *Humani Generis* §26: "Others destroy the gratuity of the supernatural order, since God, they say, cannot create intellectual beings without ordering and calling them to the beatific vision."

[293] Paschal I (817–824), in Aemilius Friedberg, ed., *Decretum Magistri Gratiani* (Leipzig: Officina Bernhardt Tauchnitz, 1889), vol. I, pars II, G. I, q. VII, c. 27. Cited in Matthew Spinka, ed., *Advocates of Reform: From Wyclif to Erasmus* (Louisville, KY: Westminster Press, 1953), 203.

[294] St Peter Damian, *The Letters of Peter Damian 121–150*, trans. Owen J. Blum (Washington, DC: Catholic University of America Press, 2004), 156.

Surely it is not without significance that it is a *Samaritan* woman with whom Jesus discusses the relative merits of finite and inexhaustible water. Indeed, the key issues at stake in the encounter between Christ and the Samaritan woman and the apostles and Simon Magus are unerringly close and the key phrase δωρεὰν τοῦ θεοῦ (the gift of God) is identical. This is why the Lord employs usury as the symbol of grace.[295] The coin of God is superabundant: the more one possesses the more one receives. The coin of Caesar is sterile. He who seeks to make it fertile gives divine honour to Caesar. "For to everyone who has will more be given, and he will have abundance; but from him who has not, even what he has will be taken away."[296] This is the practice of both God and Caesar. God has the right, Caesar does not. As Pius XI teaches, the destitute victims of the usurers will worship the state and a monster will be born: "Let all remember that Liberalism is the father of this Socialism that is pervading morality and culture and that Bolshevism will be its heir."[297]

The use of the Court of the Gentiles for profane purposes is not the only sin of the traders in the Temple. These activities themselves are said to be thievery. In the case of the money changers, that can only mean usury. It is reasonable to assume that the theft of which Christ accused the money changers in the Temple involved the charging of commission over and above their extrinsic title (i.e., their expenses). That is, it entailed

[295] It should be remembered that the Church's condemnation of usury, though a neglected teaching, is irreformably taught with the greatest solemnity. The first, tenth, eleventh, fourteenth, fifteenth, and eighteenth ecumenical councils all issued decrees on usury, but it is the ecumenical council of Vienne (1311–1312) that is at once most ferocious and most succinct: "If indeed someone has fallen into the error of presuming to affirm pertinaciously that the practice of usury is not sinful, we decree that he is to be punished as a heretic; and we strictly enjoin on local ordinaries and inquisitors of heresy to proceed against those they find suspect of such error as they would against those suspected of heresy." Tanner, *Decrees*, 1:384–85.

[296] Matthew 25:29.

[297] Pius XI, *Quadragesimo Anno* (1931) §122.

usury.[298] This of course adds particular resonance to the cleansing of the Temple in light of Psalm 14:

> O LORD, who shall sojourn in thy tent?
> Who shall dwell on thy holy hill?
> He who walks blamelessly, and does what is right,
> and speaks truth from his heart;
> who does not slander with his tongue,
> and does no evil to his friend,
> nor takes up a reproach against his neighbour;
> in whose eyes a reprobate is despised,
> but who honours those who fear the Lord;
> who swears to his own hurt and does not change;
> who does not put out his money at interest,
> and does not take a bribe against the innocent.
> He who does these things shall never be moved.

Thus, in Revelation's chapter thirteen we return once more to the Court of the Gentiles and the dispute over Caesar's tribute:

> And it was allowed to give breath to the image of the beast so that the image of the beast should even speak, and to cause those who would not worship the image of the beast to be slain. Also it causes all, both small and great, both rich and poor, both free and slave, to be marked on the right hand or the forehead, so that no one can buy or sell unless he has the mark, that is, the name of the beast or the number of its name. This calls for wisdom: let him who has understanding reckon the number of the beast, for it is a human number, its number is six hundred and sixty-six.[299]

[298] Benedict XIV, *Vix Pervenit* (1745).

[299] Revelation 13:15–18.

The image of the beast, the coin bearing Caesar's image and title, is given breath, treated as a living thing, as a divine thing that has life in itself (see John 5:26). Men, created in the image of God, are treated as lifeless units of exchange to be branded with the name of Caesar.[300]

The image of God in man is fertile even in the natural order[301] and thus it is the great mystery,[302] the sacrament of the union of Christ and the Church, of man's supernatural participation in the God Who has life in Himself.[303] Dante placed the usurers and sodomites in the same region of Hell because one had made the sterile fertile and the other the fertile sterile.[304] The Whore of Babylon is sterile. Poppaea is kicked to death by her husband while pregnant with their child.[305] Nero "married" a slave he had castrated and simultaneously "married" himself off as bride to another male lover.[306] "As it was in the days of Lot—they ate, they drank, they bought, they sold, they planted, they built, but on the day when Lot went out from Sodom fire and sulphur rained from heaven and destroyed them all—so will it be on the day when the Son of man is revealed."[307]

In his commentary on St Paul's first letter to Timothy, St Thomas explains the connection between idolatry, usury, and heresy. Seeking to

300 It is interesting that in 1 Kings 10:14, Solomon receives six hundred and sixty-six talents of gold in revenue (more than all he spent on the Temple of God); he uses the funds to build a great palace and immediately apostatizes. This is the only other scriptural appearance of the number 666.

301 See John Paul II, Audience of November 14, 1979, in *Man and Woman He Created Them: A Theology of the Body*, trans. Michael Waldstein (Boston, MA: Pauline Books & Media, 2006), 161–65.

302 Ephesians 5:32.

303 John 5:26.

304 *Inferno*, Cantos 11 and 14–17.

305 Suetonius, *The Lives of Caesars*, trans. J.C. Rolfe (Harvard: Loeb, 1997), *Life of Nero* 35.3, p. 143.

306 Ibid., *Life of Nero* 28–29, pp. 127–28.

307 Luke 17:28–30.

explain the words "the love of money is the root of all evils," St Thomas teaches that this applies not just to inordinate desire for created goods in general but to the love of money specifically because the exchangeability of money for all temporal goods imitates the divine omnipotence. He then explains why it is that "it is through this craving that some have wandered away from the faith":

> They fall first of all into spiritual harm; hence he says, "they have erred from the faith." The reason for this is that sound doctrine forbids many unlawful profits which they refuse to give up; consequently, they invent their own doctrine which creates for them a new hope of salvation. This is what usurers often do.[308]

If we see Babylon as the tyranny of idolatry, both Jewish (in rejecting the Messiah for temporal security or power) and of Rome, then the events that follow may encompass both the destruction of and the overthrow of the Temple and of Pagan Rome. The Beast—Rome and its successor states (the ten horns)—turn on the Whore "and devour her flesh and burn her up with fire."[309]

Rome and the barbarians are converted, idolatry and heresy are overthrown, and the kingship of Christ is established on earth for a thousand years. The Messiah rules the nations with the iron sceptre of Rome; the beast and the false prophet are thrown into the lake of fire. The reference to the barbarian successor states and to the division of the empire in two goes all the way back to Daniel himself, to the iron and bronze which binds the fallen tree of Nebuchadnezzar and to the two legs of the statue with their feet of clay:

---

[308] St Thomas Aquinas, *Commentary on the Letters of St Paul to the Philippians, Colossians, Thessalonians, Timothy, Titus, and Philemon* (Lander, WY: The Aquinas Institute, 2012), 331. St Thomas also affirms that simony is a heresy in *Summa theologiae* II-II, Q. 100, art. 1, ad 1.

[309] Revelation 17:16.

> And whereas you saw the feet, and the toes, part of potter's clay, and part of iron: the kingdom shall be divided, but yet it shall take its origin from the iron, according as you saw the iron mixed with the miry clay. And as the toes of the feet were part of iron, and part of clay: the kingdom shall be partly strong, and partly broken. And whereas you saw the iron mixed with miry clay, they shall be mingled indeed together with the seed of man, but they shall not stick fast one to another, as iron cannot be mixed with clay.[310]

So, the Roman empire is divided between East and West and mingled with Germans and Slavs. St Jerome, in his commentary on Daniel, is in no doubt as to the meaning of this passage:

> Now the fourth empire, which clearly refers to the Romans, is the iron empire which breaks in pieces and overcomes all others. But its feet and toes are partly of iron and partly of earthenware, a fact most clearly demonstrated at the present time. For just as there was at the first nothing stronger or hardier than the Roman realm, so also in these last days there is nothing more feeble, since we require the assistance of barbarian tribes both in our civil wars and against foreign nations. However, at the final period of all these empires of gold and silver and bronze and iron, a rock (namely, the Lord and Saviour) was cut off without hands, that is, without copulation or human seed and by birth from a virgin's womb; and after all the empires had been crushed, He became a great mountain and filled the whole earth.[311]

[310] Daniel 2:41–42.

[311] Jerome, *Commentary on Daniel*, 32 (PL 25:504).

In fact, Jerome's interpretation hit an official nerve (probably offending the half-barbarian Stilicho, the guardian and chief minister of the Western emperor Honorius) and Jerome was forced to defend himself in his commentary on Isaiah where he said that if people didn't like what he had said, they should blame Daniel, not him, and that princes should not be flattered so as to obscure the truth of Scripture. If we are to interpret Revelation in the preterist manner, then it is clearly the same events unfolding in chapter nineteen:

> Then I saw an angel standing in the sun, and with a loud voice he called to all the birds that fly in midheaven, "Come, gather for the great supper of God, to eat the flesh of kings, the flesh of captains, the flesh of mighty men, the flesh of horses and their riders, and the flesh of all men, both free and slave, both small and great." And I saw the beast and the kings of the earth with their armies gathered to make war against him who sits upon the horse and against his army. And the beast was captured, and with it the false prophet who in its presence had worked the signs by which he deceived those who had received the mark of the beast and those who worshiped its image. These two were thrown alive into the lake of fire that burns with sulphur. And the rest were slain by the sword of him who sits upon the horse, the sword that issues from his mouth; and all the birds were gorged with their flesh. Then I saw an angel coming down from heaven, holding in his hand the key of the bottomless pit and a great chain. And he seized the dragon, that ancient serpent, who is the Devil and Satan, and bound him for a thousand years, and threw him into the pit, and shut it and sealed it over him, that he should deceive the nations no more, till the thousand years were ended. After that he must be loosed for a little while.[312]

[312] Revelation 19:17–20:3.

This triumph was accomplished in three stages: the conversion of Constantine in 312, the adoption of Catholicism as the religion of the empire by Theodosius in 380, and the translation of the empire by St Leo III in 800; and as the inspired text suggests, the temporal catastrophe of the fall of Rome was crucial to its success. But while the shattering of Rome's feet of clay was necessary to destroy the idolatry of its power, the rock which broke them and then filled the world was and remains Roman. As Prudentius, a statesman and liturgical poet in the administration of Theodosius, observed:

> What is the secret of Rome's historical destiny? It is that God wills the unity of mankind, since the religion of Christ demands a social foundation of peace and international amity. Hitherto the whole earth from east to west had been rent asunder by continual strife. To curb this madness God has taught the nations to be obedient to the same laws and all to become Romans. Now we see mankind living as citizens of one city and members of a common household. Men come from distant lands across the seas to one common forum, the peoples are united by commerce and intermarriage. From the intermingling of peoples a single race is born. This is the meaning of all the victories and triumphs of the Roman Empire: the Roman peace has prepared the road for the coming of Christ.[313]

[313] Prudentius, *Contra Symmachum*, quoted in Christopher Dawson, *The Making of Europe* (London: Sheed and Ward, 1932), 32; Prudentius, *[Works of] Prudentius*, vol. 2, trans. H.J. Thomson (Cambridge: Harvard University Press, 1949), 54–56.

5

How the Church Is Roman

ONE HUNDRED YEARS before the conversion of Constantine, the emperor Caracalla issued a constitution extending Roman citizenship to all freeborn men in the empire.[314] The beneficent act of philanthropy was probably inspired by a desire to extend the tax base, but the effect was to extend not only Roman Law but also the obligation to worship the Roman gods to all its beneficiaries.[315] This transformed the nature of the offence given by Christians to the civil order from a generic act of impiety to a specific failure to uphold the cult upon which the safety of the Roman Commonwealth relied. In the course of the third century, Persia re-emerged as a great power in the world and a genuine threat to the external security of the empire. This transformation stretched the resources of the Roman state to the limit. The constant pressure of barbarian migration and the menace of the Sassanids were too much for the resources of the Roman state as then organised.[316] The fiscal exactions of the central government had to grow considerably, and the centre of institutional gravity shifted not only from the civilian to the military (a process already well under way) but also from

[314] Paul Keresztes, "The *Constitutio Antoniniana* and the Persecutions under Caracalla," in *The American Journal of Philology*, vol. 91, no. 4 (October 1970): 446–59.

[315] Elizabeth DePalma Digeser, *The Making of a Christian Empire: Lactantius and Rome* (Ithaca, NY: Cornell University Press, 2000).

[316] Peter Heather, *The Fall of the Roman Empire: A New History of Rome and the Barbarians* (Oxford: Oxford University Press, 2006).

the geographical centre to the frontier. This transformation, while arguably necessary, strengthened the destabilising tendency for the imperial office to be transmitted by a series of coups and for different frontier regions to raise up usurpers in the hope of obtaining some of the benefits bestowed by the proximity of the imperial administration. In order to counter these tendencies, an effort was made under Diocletian, the emperor who is considered to have resolved this "third-century crisis," to create a college of emperors and a new coherent and integrated imperial religious ideology.

Diocletian transformed the imperial office, assuming the title Dominus (or Kyrios) and demanding prostration from his "subjects." He associated himself with the traditional head of the Roman pantheon, Jupiter, and his colleague Maximian with Hercules, and officially attributed to himself divine honours. These were actions previously undertaken only by a few of the mentally unstable emperors of the first century. They constituted the beginning of a new era in imperial history, a period known as the Dominate, as opposed to the Principate instituted by Augustus in 27 BC in which the emperor remained a magistrate of the Republic, one citizen among theoretical equals.[317]

While this institutional revolution was underway, a philosophical revolution was also beginning which would have profound repercussions for the ancient world and its successor cultures. In Alexandria the dockyard worker Ammonius Saccas (active 232–243) initiated the movement known as Neo-Platonism. Unlike earlier philosophical movements in the ancient world, the Neo-Platonists did not assert or imply a critique of the religion of the time but attempted to reinterpret it as a form of picture language for their own philosophy. This was true not only of Paganism but also of Christianity—for not only Plotinus but also Origen sat at the feet of Ammonius Saccas. The two men shared a belief crucial to the Platonism of late antiquity (though seemingly absent from Plato's *Timaeus*) that, in

[317] George Mousourakis, *A Legal History of Rome* (Routledge: Abingdon, 2007), 135–42.

Origen's words, "God cannot be called omnipotent unless there exist those over whom He may exercise His power; and therefore, that God may be shown to be almighty, it is necessary that all things should exist."[318] The first being is beyond being and is alone Good. The *ratio* of the Good is to diffuse itself and consequently the first being must diffuse Himself infinitely. For orthodox Christianity this occurs through the begetting of the Son and the procession of the Spirit; for Origen and Plotinus it occurs through the emanation of all possible entities, beginning with a gradation of "divine" beings who in the thought of Origen substitute for the Blessed Trinity. Likewise, the return of all things to the One from which they came is a necessity for the disciples of Ammonius Saccas, while for the Church, just as God is a Trinity of coequal persons, so the generation of creatures is a free act of creation, and the supernatural order gratuitous and enjoyed ultimately only by a few.[319]

[318] ". . . ne omnipotens quidem Deus dici potest, si non sint, in quos exerceat potentatum: et ideo ut omnipotens ostendatur Deus, omnia subsistere necesse est" (PG 11:139). Trans. F. Crombie, in *ANF*, vol. 4 (Buffalo, NY: Christian Literature Publishing Co., 1885), 249–50.

[319] "As we have seen, a division between natural and supernatural would be meaningless in Plotinus's systems, whereas in Augustine's it is the basic framework of metaphysics." Leszek Kołakowski, *Main Currents of Marxism* (New York: W. W. Norton & Company, 2008), 17. Porphyry chillingly explains how Origen used Christianity as a picture language for Neo-Platonic thought, even as his pagan comrades sought to do with the Hellenic myths. "As an example of this absurdity take a man whom I met when I was young, and who was then greatly celebrated and still is, on account of the writings which he has left. I refer to Origen, who is highly honoured by the teachers of these doctrines. For this man, having been a student of Ammonius, who had attained the greatest proficiency in philosophy of any in our day, derived much benefit from his teacher in the knowledge of the sciences; but as to the correct choice of life, he pursued a course opposite to his. For Ammonius, being a Christian, and brought up by Christian parents, when he gave himself to study and to philosophy straightway conformed to the life required by the laws. But Origen, having been educated as a Greek in Greek literature, went over to the barbarian recklessness. And carrying over the learning which he had obtained, he hawked it about, in his life conducting himself as a Christian and

While Origen was excommunicated by St Demetrius of Alexandria in 231 (a measure recognised and endorsed in Rome), he was enthusiastically embraced by the bishops of the Holy Land. Indeed, it was their irregular ordination of a eunuch subject to another bishop that triggered the excommunication.[320] This admiration for the rogue Alexandrian was passed down to bishop Eusebius of Caesarea who would become the Eastern apologist of the new Christian empire in the fourth century.[321] But before this could happen, the disciples of Ammonius had already established themselves as the interpreters of the new order of the Roman world at the Pagan court of Diocletian himself. Here Porphyry, the disciple and biographer of Plotinus, lectured on the new synthesis of Platonism and traditional Paganism and exhorted the college of emperors to turn upon the Christians with a new vigour and severity, climaxing in 303 with the Great Persecution. The

contrary to the laws, but in his opinions of material things and of the Deity being like a Greek, and mingling Grecian teachings with foreign fables. For he was continually studying Plato, and he busied himself with the writings of Numenius and Cronius, Apollophanes, Longinus, Moderatus, and Nicomachus, and those famous among the Pythagoreans. And he used the books of Chaeremon the Stoic, and of Cornutus. Becoming acquainted through them with the figurative interpretation of the Grecian mysteries, he applied it to the Jewish Scriptures." Eusebius, *Church History*, in *NPNF* II, vol. 1, ed. P. Schaff and H. Wace (Grand Rapids, MI: Wm. B. Eerdmans, 1955), 265–66.

320 It can scarcely be a coincidence, especially given the key role of the anti-Origenist St Eustathius of Antioch at the council, that the first disciplinary canon of Nicaea reads: "If anyone in sickness has undergone surgery at the hands of physicians or has been castrated by barbarians, let him remain among the clergy. But if anyone in good health has castrated himself, if he is enrolled among the clergy he should be suspended, and in future no such man should be promoted. But, as it is evident that this refers to those who are responsible for the condition and presume to castrate themselves, so too if any have been made eunuchs by barbarians or by their masters, but have been found worthy, the canon admits such men to the clergy." Tanner, *Decrees*, 1:6.

321 "For the Greek of the Hellenistic age, the king had been transformed into a god among men; Eusebius had only to drop the godhead of the king and put in its place the Vicegerent of God: Constantine." Norman H. Baynes, *Byzantine Studies and Other Essays* (London: Athlone Press, 1955), 48.

principle of the necessity of the generation of all possible entities has political as well as metaphysical consequences.[322] By denying freedom to the "creator" and plurality to the Godhead, it establishes unity alone as the criterion of perfection, creating a sort of reverse principle of subsidiarity: if two social entities can equally well perform the same function, the greater and not the lesser should do it. This was the perfect rationale for the increasingly totalitarian turn taken by the Roman empire.[323] When the pagan expression of this creed was overthrown by the victorious Constantine, Eusebius of Caesarea was on hand to proffer a "Christian" alternative.[324]

---

[322] Malcolm Barber, *Two Cities: Medieval Europe, 1050–1320* (London: Routledge, 2004), 375.

[323] Kołakowski rightly traces the genealogy of Marxism, the defining totalitarianism of the twentieth century, to Plotinus's thought and notes that the essential difference between the thought of Augustine and that of Neo-Platonism lies in the former's being "based on the Incarnation and Redemption and the idea of a personal God who calls the world into being by his own free choice." This, Kołakowski notes, represents a firm rejection by Augustine of the Alexandrian heresiarch: "he expresses astonishment at what he calls Origen's errors on the subject. God, he [Augustine] declares, does not experience any lack; the creation is the effect of his goodness; he did not create the world from necessity or from any need of his own, but because he is good and because it is fitting for the Supreme Good to create good things." See *Main Currents of Marxism*, 10–21.

[324] "Eastern Christianity had grown up at the cross-roads of Hellenistic and Oriental culture. It had absorbed something from both—sufficient, indeed, to cause some to hold that the historic facts of the faith, uncomfortable facts, had been lost sight off. East Roman Christians saw the Kingdom of God on earth as a symbol of the Kingdom of heaven and only secondarily as an historic reality valid because of the facts of the Incarnation and the Resurrection. The greatest of the Eastern Fathers, Origen of Caesarea, had laid himself open to attack on these grounds. One critic, Porphyry, even argued that though he was Christian in the manner of his life he was Hellene in his religious thought and adapted Neo-Platonism to the interpretation of the Scriptures. This, of course, was gross over-simplification; Origen was one of a select company whose works taught Christians not to be afraid of pagan culture; but it had a germ of truth in it. Another Caesarean, Eusebius, took Origen's Christianity one stage further on its journey as a political and social force in writings that exercised a profound influence

And yet, the first language of Constantine was not Greek but Latin. When he was compelled to flee from the court of Diocletian's successor in Nicomedia in 305, he had been preceded into the West by another Latin: the orator and Christian Lactantius, whom Constantine would eventually establish as tutor to his son Crispus. Lactantius was no enthusiast for the new imperial ideology in either its Christian or its Pagan form. Instead of the Dominate he proposed a return to the Principate of Augustus, contrasting the impiety of Jove, with whom the senior emperor now associated himself, with the golden age of Saturn with which the Augustan age was identified by Virgil in the fourth Eclogue (ever popular among Christians). He had no time for those who offered *proskynesis* to the emperors: "For whosoever shall cast away the conduct becoming a man, and, following present things, shall prostrate himself upon the ground, will be punished as a deserter from his Lord, his commander, and his Father."[325]

Whether intentionally or unintentionally, Constantine the Great would strike two mighty blows for the Roman tradition of republicanism. First, there was his traditional acclamation as emperor at York (Eboracum) in 306, which, due to his final triumphant attainment of sole rule over the empire after the Battle of Chrysopolis on September 18, 324, destroyed the "Tetrarchy": Diocletian's attempt to substitute an emanationist self-legitimising transmission of power for the sovereignty of the senate and the people of Rome. Second, his foundation of Constantinople established a capital so perfectly located and so utterly impregnable that never again could a pure military coup establish an emperor without the consent of the civilian population (elite and plebeian) of the metropolis.

---

upon the emperors. The Roman emperor, for Eusebius, was the Expected One, the David of Christian prophecy, and his Empire the Messianic Kingdom." J.M. Wallace-Hadrill, *The Barbarian West 400–1000* (Oxford: Blackwell, 1985), 13.

[325] Lactantius, *Divine Institutes*, 7:27, trans. W. Fletcher, in *ANF*, vol. 7 (Buffalo, NY: Christian Literature Publishing Co., 1886), 223.

There is a mysterious prophecy of the establishment of Constantinople and all it would represent by Aristotle in Book 7, chapter 7 of his *Politics*:

> Those who live in a cold climate and in Europe are full of spirit, but wanting in intelligence and skill; and therefore they retain comparative freedom, but have no political organization, and are incapable of ruling over others. Whereas the natives of Asia are intelligent and inventive, but they are wanting in spirit, and therefore they are always in a state of subjection and slavery. But the Hellenic race, which is situated between them, is likewise intermediate in character, being high-spirited and also intelligent. Hence it continues free, and is the best-governed of any nation, and, if it could be formed into one state, would be able to rule the world.[326]

The greatest of all bishops of Constantinople, St John Chrysostom himself, would expound in his twenty-third Homily on Romans the golden mean between contractualist popular sovereignty and divine-right monarchy, the antagonism between which would devastate Europe in the seventeenth century:

> "For there is no power," [St Paul] says, "but of God." What say you? It may be said; is every ruler then elected by God? This I do not say, he answers. Nor am I now speaking about individual rulers, but about the thing in itself. For that there should be rulers, and some rule and others be ruled, and that all things should not just be carried on in one confusion, the people swaying like waves in this direction and that; this, I say, is the work of God's wisdom. Hence he does not say, "for there is no ruler but of God"; but it is the thing he speaks of, and says, "there is no power but of God. And the powers that be, are ordained of God." Thus when a certain wise

[326] Aristotle, *Politics* (Mineola, NY: Dover Publications, 2000).

> man says, "It is by the Lord that a man is matched with a woman" (Proverbs 19:14 LXX), he means this, God made marriage, and not that it is He that joins together every man that comes to be with a woman.[327]

And yet the counterinfluence of Origen lived on. Lactantius had far more real intimacy with Constantine than Eusebius ever did, but sometime after the emperor's conquest of the East in 324 the orator disappears from history. His pupil, the emperor's eldest son Crispus, was put to death by his father in 326 as a result of a deception perpetrated by his stepmother Fausta which remained undiscovered until too late. The court and the dynasty fell increasingly under Eusebius's ally, namesake, and fellow Origenist Eusebius of Nicomedia. While the Council of Nicaea was firmly in the hands of figures such as Eustathius of Antioch, hostile to the Alexandrian heresiarch and thus confirmed the basis of Origen's excommunication in its canons, after a brief period of exile for resisting Nicaea Eusebius of Nicomedia was able to return and together with his colleague in Caesarea procure the banishment of St Eustathius and obtain the See of Constantinople for himself. It would be Eusebius of Nicomedia who baptised Constantine on his deathbed in 337 and a year later Eusebius of Caesarea published the "authorised version" of the emperor's life. Constantius II resolutely upheld an Arian position until his death and Eusebius of Nicomedia's pupil Julian abandoned Christianity altogether when he succeeded to the purple in 361.

Eusebius of Caesarea and Lactantius express a divergence already firmly in place at the beginning of the fourth century between two understandings of how the Church is Roman. This divergence would be vastly reinforced by the fall of the empire in the West, a process that began while the ink was still wet on the page of Prudentius's enthusiastic outburst (quoted

[327] PG 60:616. Trans. J. Walker, J. Sheppard, and H. Browne, in *NPNF* I, vol. 11 (Buffalo, NY: Christian Literature Publishing Co., 1889).

at the end of the last chapter), when, in the year 405 or 406, the Rhine froze and the Vandals, Alans, and Suebi flooded across a Roman frontier which would never be restored.[328] Less than five years later, Rome herself would be sacked for the first time in eight hundred years. Sixty-six years later the Roman Senate wrote to the emperor in Constantinople informing him there was no further need for an emperor in the West.[329] The Eastern emperor would now be recognised as the sole ruler of the Roman world, exercising his nominal authority through the barbarian kings between whom the Latin speaking regions of the Ecumene had been divided.

These events would have a profound effect on the Western understanding of *Romanitas* and its role in the identity of the Church. They ended the unified conversation of the Mediterranean world by diminishing and then extinguishing Greek literacy in the West and then Latin literacy in the East. Hostility to Origen would eventually be far more stridently expressed in the East where no less than four ecumencial councils would condemn his "mythical speculations" and "useless knowledge," but this was in many ways a reflection of the shadow he still cast there.[330] Cut off from Greek and endowed with the towering figure of St Augustine, the West was entirely emancipated intellectually from the Alexandrian. Augustine was also the author of the great theological answer to the questions raised by the sack of Rome, the *City of God*. A comparison of the doctrine of this *magnum opus et arduum* with that

[328] See Jerome, *Epistle* 123 (PL 22:1046–59), trans. W.H. Fremantle, G. Lewis, and W.G. Martley, in *NPNF* II, vol. 6 (Buffalo, NY: Christian Literature Publishing Co., 1893), 230–38.

[329] Colin D. Gordon, *The Age of Attila: Fifth-Century Byzantium and the Barbarians* (Ann Arbor, MI: University of Michigan Press, 2013), 127.

[330] Origen would eventually be condemned by a fifth ecumenical council, that of Florence in 1442, but as this was a reunion council with the dissident Eastern churches (specifically the Copts in this instance), it is the exception which proves the rule. See Tanner, *Decrees*, 1:580.

of Eusebius of Caesarea's *Oration in Praise of Constantine* dramatically illustrates the two visions.[331]

For Eusebius, the monarchy of the emperor is an image of the rule of the Logos Himself over the kosmos, the viceregent of the monarchy of the Father who alone is true God. As the Logos is living law, a sort of blueprint or instrumental formal cause through which God fashions and governs all things, so the emperor is the living principle of unity within the universal dominion of the Romans. Forms of government other than monarchy are madness.[332] The prophecy that the saints of the Most High shall inherit the kingdom is fulfilled in the government of Constantine and his appointment of various relatives to positions of office within the imperial administration. The vision of the New Jerusalem descending from heaven at the end of Revelation is fulfilled in the construction of the Basilica of the Holy Sepulchre in Jerusalem.[333] Eschatology is realised fully in the Chris-

331 See the famous essay by Erik Peterson: "Monotheism as a Political Problem," in *Theological Tractates* (Stanford, CA: Stanford University Press, 2011), 68–105.

332 "Lastly, invested as he is with a semblance of heavenly sovereignty, he directs his gaze above, and frames his earthly government according to the pattern of that Divine original, feeling strength in its conformity to the monarchy of God. And this conformity is granted by the universal Sovereign to man alone of the creatures of this earth: for he only is the author of sovereign power, who decrees that all should be subject to the rule of one. And surely monarchy far transcends every other constitution and form of government: for that democratic equality of power, which is its opposite, may rather be described as anarchy and disorder. Hence there is one God, and not two, or three, or more: for to assert a plurality of gods is plainly to deny the being of God at all. There is one Sovereign; and his Word and royal Law is one: a Law not expressed in syllables and words, not written or engraved on tablets, and therefore subject to the ravages of time; but the living and self-subsisting Word, who himself is God, and who administers his Father's kingdom on behalf of all who are after him and subject to his power." Eusebius of Caesarea, *De Laudibus Constantini* 1:3 (PG 20:1329–32), trans. E.C. Richardson, *NPNF* II, vol. 1 (Buffalo, NY: Christian Literature Publishing Co., 1890), 584.

333 Eusebius, *De Vita Constantini* 3:33 (PG 20:1093–95); *De Laudibus Constantini* 1:3 (PG 20:1329–30).

tianised Roman state. So successful was Eusebius's "realised eschatology" of the empire that only one commentary would ever be written on the book of Revelation by an orthodox writer in the East[334] before the fall of Constantinople in 1453—and that, only at the lowest ebb of the empire at the beginning of the seventh century. The Book of Revelation did not feature at all in the Byzantine liturgy.[335] On one point only did Eusebius agree with the later analysis of Augustine: he denied the legitimacy of any non-Christian government and so implied that a substantial change had occurred in the Roman polity after 312. This understanding is reflected in a dispute in the ninth century between St Cyril and the rabbis of the Crimea. St Cyril (then still Constantine the Philosopher) was challenged on how it could be that Jesus is the Messiah when Daniel tells us that the coming of the Messiah will mark the end of the fourth monarchy (which all agree is the Roman empire) and its replacement by a fifth. Was not Cyril a Roman sent from the empire which endured to that day? Cyril denies that he is, in this sense, a Roman. The pagan empire of antiquity has perished; the Roman empire of his day is the kingdom of Messiah.

> [The Roman Empire] does not retain [its dominion] for it is gone just as the others according to the image in the vision. Now our Kingdom is not Roman but Christ's, as the prophet said: "The God

[334] Andrew of Caesarea.

[335] One nineteenth-century defender of Eusebius would go as far as to say: "I need now only say, all these things have been done: the old and elementary system passed away with a great noise; all these predicted empires have actually fallen, and the new kingdom, the new heaven and earth, the new Jerusalem—all of which were to descend from God, to be formed by His power, have been realised on earth; all these things have been done in the sight of all the nations; God's holy arm has been made bare in their sight: His judgments have prevailed, and they remain for an everlasting testimony to the whole world. His kingdom has come, as it was foretold it should, and His will has, so far, been done." Samuel Lee, *Eusebius of Caesarea. The Theophania or Divine Manifestation of Our Lord and Saviour Jesus Christ* (Cambridge: Cambridge University Press, 1843), cli.

> of Heaven shall set up a kingdom, which shall never be destroyed: and His kingdom shall not be left to another people, but it shall stand forever." For is it not a Christian kingdom that is now called by Christ's name? The Romans, however, revered idols. But they—now from one tribe, now from another—rule in the name of Christ.[336]

This reflected the understanding not only of Eusebius but of Constantine the Great who had quoted the fourth Eclogue in his "Address to the Assembly of the Saints" to show the providential coincidence of the empire and the Incarnation.[337]

Very different was the approach of Augustine. He divided the human race exhaustively into the City of God inspired by the love of God to the contempt of self, and the City of the World founded by the love of self to point of contempt for God.[338] These two cities both found their expression in mankind from the moment of Cain's fratricide. The fratricide of Romulus recapitulates this, underlining the manner in which pagan Rome embodies the City of the World. For while Abel belonged to the heavenly city, Remus differed from his brother only insofar as he failed. The City of God is not the Christian empire of Constantine but the Catholic Church.[339] There is a resemblance between the City of Rome formed out of escaped criminals and the Church founded out of forgiven sinners, and the promises made to Rome in legend are fulfilled in the Church, but the Roman dominion has been (as Aquinas too will later assert) translated into the spiritual order.

---

336 "Life of Constantine the Philosopher," in Marvin Kantor, *Medieval Slavic Studies of Saints and Princes*, Michigan Slavic Publications (Ann Arbor, MI: The University of Michigan, 1983), 53.

337 PG 20:1233–1316.

338 St Augustine, *De Civitate Dei*, 14.28. "Fecerunt itaque ciuitates duas amores duo, terrenam scilicet amor sui usque ad contemptum Dei, caelestem uero amor Dei usque ad contemptum sui."

339 *City of God* 13.16.

> In former times you had glory from the peoples, but, through the inscrutable decision of divine providence, the true religion was not there for you to choose. Awake! The day has come. You have already awakened in the persons of some of your people, in whose perfect virtue we Christians boast, and even in their suffering for the true faith; they have wrestled everywhere against hostile powers, have conquered them by the courage of their deaths, and "have won this country for us by their blood."
>
> It is to this country that we invite you, and exhort you to add yourself to the number of our citizens. The refuge we offer is the true remission of sins. Do not listen to those degenerate sons of yours who disparage Christ and the Christians, and criticize these times as an unhappy age, when the kind of period they would like is one which offers not a life of tranquillity but security for their vicious pursuits. Such satisfactions have never been enough for you, even in respect of your earthly country. Now take possession of the Heavenly Country, for which you will have to endure but little hardship; and you will reign there in truth and for ever. There you will find no Vestal hearth, no Capitoline stone, but the one true God, who fixes no bounds for you of space or time but will bestow an empire without end.[340]

In the West, therefore, the locus of *Romanitas* was felt less and less to be the emperor on the Bosporus, who adopted Greek as the imperial language in 629 and by the ninth century could unblushingly describe Latin as a barbarous and Scythic tongue.[341] The Holy See was now seen as the guarantor of the Roman character of Christendom. This growing conviction of the Western barbarians was long anticipated by the popes

[340] *City of God* 2.29, trans. H. Bettenson (London: Penguin, 1984), 86–87.

[341] Kallistos Ware, *The Orthodox Church* (London: Penguin Books, 1993), 46.

themselves. In his eighty-second sermon (for the Feast of Ss Peter and Paul), St Leo the Great presents a picture of the relationship between the dominion of Rome and the Messianic kingdom very different from that of St Cyril:

> For [the apostles Peter and Paul] are the men, through whom the light of Christ's gospel shone on you, O Rome, and through whom you, who wast the teacher of error, wast made the disciple of Truth. These are your holy Fathers and true shepherds, who gave you claims to be numbered among the heavenly kingdoms, and built you under much better and happier auspices than [Romulus and Remus], by whose zeal the first foundations of your walls were laid: and of whom the one that gave you your name defiled you with his brother's blood. These are they who promoted you to such glory, that being made a holy nation, a chosen people, a priestly and royal state, and the head of the world through the blessed Peter's holy See you attained a wider sway by the worship of God than by earthly government. For although you were increased by many victories, and extended your rule on land and sea, yet what your toils in war subdued is less than what the peace of Christ has conquered.[342]

For the Byzantines, the Roman empire endures but no longer in the city of Rome: it has passed across the Adriatic to Byzantium and has become the Messianic kingdom. For Pope Leo the Great, the dominion of Rome also continues—but remains upon the Tiber where, though her temporal empire has passed away, she reigns as the iron sceptre of the Son of Man through the Holy See of Peter.[343]

---

[342] Leo the Great, *Sermon* 82 (PL 54:422–23), trans. C.L. Feltoe, in *NPNF* II, vol. 12 (Buffalo, NY: Christian Literature Publishing Co., 1895), 194–95.

[343] Aidan Nichols, *Rome and the Eastern Churches: A Study in Schism* (San Francisco: Ignatius Press, 2010), 315.

But why does Leo even bother? It is easy to see why St Cyril as a loyal Byzantine needs to defend the function of the empire in the workings of Providence; but St Leo, who only just managed to turn Attila the Hun from the gates of Rome and would live to see the Vandals plunder the Capitol—why should he care to preserve the fourth monarchy in existence, albeit in a spiritual form? Cynically, one might suggest that the Roman pontiff could not afford to dislodge the Eternal City from its central position in history and providence. Yet the Petrine mandate in and of itself would seem enough to secure his position; why, then, exclude a translation of the papal see on principle? In a sense, more important than any other consideration was the restraining power mentioned in 2 Thessalonians 2, for this meant that the same power which restrained then must restrain until the end. In fact, as early as the *Letter of Barnabas*[344] the idea had taken hold (unofficially and subject to official disapproval) that the history of the world would last only six thousand years.[345] Lactantius in the *Divine Institutes* affirms both that the end would come after the sixth millennium and that it would be preceded by the fall of Rome:

> I have already shown above, that when six thousand years shall be completed this change must take place, and that the last day of the extreme conclusion is now drawing near . . . the fall and ruin of the world will shortly take place; except that while the city of Rome remains it appears that nothing of this kind is to be feared. But when that capital of the world shall have fallen, and shall have begun to be a street, which the Sibyls say shall come to pass, who can doubt that the end has now arrived to the affairs of men and the

[344] *Letter to Barnabas* 16:4, in Louth, *Early Christian Writings*, 153.

[345] Richard Landes, "Lest the Millennium Be Fulfilled: Apocalyptic Expectations and the Pattern of Western Chronography 100–800," in Werner Verbeke, Daniel Verhelst, and Andries Welkenhuysen, eds., *The Use and Abuse of Eschatology in the Middle Ages* (Leuven: Leuven University Press, 1988), 137–211.

> whole world? It is that city, that only, which still sustains all things; and the God of heaven is to be entreated by us and implored—if, indeed, His arrangements and decrees can be delayed—lest, sooner than we think that detestable tyrant should come.[346]

Although according to the Hebrew text of the Old Testament employed by St Jerome in the Vulgate this would mean the end times would begin in the 1990s,[347] the most popular chronological system in both East and West until the *Anno Domini* took over under the Carolingians was that employed by Eusebius (and ironically by Jerome himself in his *Chronicon*),[348] which dated the year six thousand A.M. [*anno mundi*] much earlier, to AD 801.

The Donation of Constantine, a forgery of the eighth century, already laid the groundwork for the conception of a western Christendom in which the pope is the universal principle of unity and the kings reign

[346] PL 6:812–13. Trans. W. Fletcher, in *ANF*, vol. 7 (Buffalo, NY: Christian Literature Publishing Co., 1886), 220. "Iam superius ostendi, completis annorum sex millibus mutationem istam fieri oportere, et iam propinquare summum illum conclusionis extremae diem . . . lapsum ruinamque rerum brevi fore: nisi quod incolumi urbe Roma nihil istismodi videtur esse metuendum. At vero cum caput illud orbis occiderit, et Ρύμη esse coeperit, quod Sibyllae fore aiunt, quis dubitet venisse iam finem rebus humanis, orbique terrarum? Illa, illa est civitas, quae adhuc sustentat omnia; precandusque nobis et adorandus est Deus coeli; si tamen statuta eius et placita differi possunt, ne citius quam putemus tyrannus ille abominabilis veniat."

[347] The popular early modern biblical chronology of James Ussher, Protestant "bishop" of Armagh, placed the creation in the year at 4004 BC and so the fateful sixth millennium in 1996. J. Ussher, *Annales Veteris Testamenti, a prima mundi origine deducti una cum rerum asiaticarum et aegyptiacarum chronico, a temporis historici principio usque ad . . . /Jacobo Usserio Armachano digestore* (London: E. Tyler, 1658). St Bede calculated 3952 BC, although he would go on to strongly discourage millenarian speculation. *On the Nature of Things; And, On Times*, trans. C. B. Kendall, and F. Wallis (Liverpool: Liverpool University Press, 2010).

[348] Although Eusebius and Jerome compare the several versions beginning at PL 27:57.

beneath him and at his sufferance.[349] It is often speculated that this was shown to Pepin the Short when he bestowed the Papal States on Pope Stephen II in 754 and in justification of Pepin's own papally warranted deposition of the last Merovingian king of the Franks.[350] Be that as it may, the use of this text to buttress papal claims was relatively rare. By the eleventh century, a fully worked-out doctrine of universal papal dominion in Spirituals immediately and Temporals by delegation was in operation, grounded upon Scripture and with no suggestion that this was the gift of Constantine or that it was confined to the West. The full rigor of this doctrine would be solemnly[351] defined by Pope Boniface VIII in the 1302 Bull *Unam Sanctam*.[352]

Were it not for the continuing military decline of Byzantium and the faulty chronology of Eusebius and Jerome's *Chronicon*, here matters might have rested with a Western doctrine of a papal *Romanitas* and an Eastern doctrine of an imperial church. Instead, the hysteria surrounding the year 6000 A.M. and the coming of the antichrist precipitated a crisis which would expose the divergent understandings of ecclesiastical *Romanitas* in East and West and paradoxically offer a theoretical resolution. Ironically, so long as the pope remained within the Byzantine empire (however autonomously) and the emperor remained in communion with Rome, the divergence remained submerged. This solution slipped away when Pepin endowed the popes with an independent sovereignty over central Italy. From this point unity with the East was actually assisted by heresy in

---

349 Robert Foltz, *The Concept of Empire in Western Europe from the Fifth to the Fourteenth Century* (London: Edward Arnold, 1969), 10–12; idem, *The Coronation of Charlemagne, 25 December 800* (London: Routledge and Kegan Paul, 1974), 109–11; 169–70.

350 Paul Edward Dutton, ed., *Carolingian Civilization* (Peterborough, ON: Broadview, 1993), 13–19.

351 See Pius XII, *Mystici Corporis* §40; see John P. Joy, *Disputed Questions on Papal Infallibility* (Lincoln, NE: Os Justi Press, 2022), 98–101.

352 DH 870–75.

the East for, while Rome still exercised its function of rock of orthodoxy and the emperors were iconoclasts, the Christological breach distracted attention from the ecclesiological problem while reinforcing the loyalty of the iconodules to the Holy See.

In 787 at the Second Council of Nicaea, the iconoclastic controversy was, at least temporarily, resolved. The emperor Leo IV had died young in 780 and his widow Irene as regent for her son Constantine VI had come to power in Constantinople. Irene was orthodox and was resolved to ensure the triumph of the venerators of icons. It was under her auspices (with papal legates) that the seventh ecumencial council had been held at Nicaea in 787.[353] However, in 790 Constantine VI tired of serving under his mother as regent and removed her from office, taking power for himself. In 795 there was a change of pope in Rome. The long-reigning Adrian I had died and Pope St Leo III was elected to replace him. Adrian having had further problems with the Lombards of northern Italy had once again had to call upon the help of the new Frankish ruler Charles the Great (or Charlemagne), son of Pepin the Short. Charlemagne had ultimately abolished the Lombard kingdom and annexed it to his own domains which now encompassed all of Christian mainland Western Europe not in Muslim hands. That is, Charlemagne now ruled as much of the ancient Western empire as the emperor in Constantinople did of the ancient Eastern empire. The pope had bestowed upon him the Roman title of "Patrician" in order that he might receive proper honours when visiting the City.[354]

One of the problems attendant upon the new temporal power of the popes was that the stakes in papal elections had risen.[355] Factional violence was now far more likely to break out over a papal election and this was

---

[353] Tanner, *Decrees*, 1:131–32.

[354] Roger Collins, *Charlemagne* (Toronto: University of Toronto Press, 1998), 39, 60, 72.

[355] Peter Heather, *The Restoration of Rome: Barbarian Popes and Imperial Pretenders* (London: MacMillan, 2013), 299–348.

what did indeed now happen with disturbing frequency.[356] The family of Adrian I were not happy that he had not been succeeded by one of their own and tempers simmered. Slanderous claims against Pope Leo III were circulated in Rome.[357]

Meanwhile in Constantinople, frustrated at her removal from office and suspicious that her son harboured Iconoclastic sympathies, Irene was plotting her return to power. In a horrific incident in 797, Irene captured her son and blinded him in the very chamber in which she had given birth to him. He died of his injuries. Irene, aware that in Roman law a woman could not rule,[358] declared herself "emperor" (Basileus, not Basilissa).[359] The Westerners, who still technically lived as part of the world-order of which the emperor was head, were not convinced. But as these dramatic events were unfolding on the Bosphorus, the other pillar of the Christian world-order was suddenly overturned in Rome.

The relatives of Adrian I attacked Leo III during a procession through the streets of the Eternal City in April 799; the pope was attacked, his eyes gouged out, and his tongue removed. He was declared deposed and sent off to a monastery. Unfortunately for his enemies, Leo's eyes and tongue were restored by a miracle and he escaped from the monastery and fled across the Alps to Charlemagne.[360]

It is very difficult for us now to appreciate the disorientation these events caused in the eighth century. The simultaneous vacancy of both the See of Rome and the Roman empire through violence and usurpation was

---

356 Nichols, *Rome and the Eastern Churches*, 220.

357 Heather, *Restoration*, 244.

358 "Feminae ab omnibus officiis civilibus vel publicis remotae sunt et ideo nec iudices esse possunt nec magistratum gerere nec postulare nec pro alio intervenire nec procuratores existere." Ulpian, *Digest*, 50.17.2.

359 She continued to use the feminine title as well.

360 James Bryce, *The Holy Roman Empire* (London: MacMillan, 1895), 44; P.D. King, *Charlemagne* (London: Routledge, 1986), 37.

a terrifying event. Both the guarantors of ecclesiastical *Romanitas* were overthrown. Whether one took the Eastern or Western view of what it was that restrained the coming of Antichrist, that restraint had been removed—and with less than two years to go before the dreaded year 6000 A.M.[361]

What occurred in consequence was "one of those very few events of which, taking them singly, it may be said that if they had not happened, the history of the world would have been different."[362] Charlemagne's advisor Alcuin of York wrote to the Frankish king underlining the gravity of the situation and pointing out that, with both pope and emperor deposed, the safety of the Christian people now rested on him alone.[363] Charlemagne temporarily set aside his incessant wars with the Saxons and travelled to Rome with St Leo III. On the principle that no one on earth may judge the pope, Leo III purged himself of the charges brought against him by his opponents by means of an oath. At the council called to witness this oath his enemies were condemned in his stead. The assembled fathers and the people besought Charles, "as the name of emperor had now ceased in the land of the Greeks," to assume it himself. Charles acceded to their request. On December 25, 800 (which was then New Year's day, and so the first day of 801 in the year 6000 A.M. according to the Eusebian reckoning) Charles attended Pontifical Mass in St Peter's Basilica:

> And then the gracious and venerable pontiff with his own hands crowned him [Charles] with a very precious crown. Then all the faithful people of Rome, seeing the defense that he gave and the love that he bore for the holy Roman Church and her Vicar, by the will of God and of the blessed Peter, the keeper of the keys of the kingdom of heaven, cried with one accord in a loud voice:

[361] Landes, *Lest the Millennium*, 200; Nicols, *Rome and the Eastern Churches*, 239. The Carolingians were still convinced the end was imminent eight years later.

[362] Bryce, *Holy Roman Empire*, 52.

[363] *Alcuin of York*, trans. S. Allot (York: Ebor Press, 1974), 111.

> "To Charles, the most pious Augustus, crowned by God, the great and peace-giving emperor, life and victory." While he was invoking diverse saints before the holy confession of the blessed Peter the Apostle, it was proclaimed three times and he was constituted by all to be emperor of the Romans. Then the most holy pontiff anointed Charles with holy oil, and likewise anointed his most excellent son to be king, upon the very day of the birth of our Lord Jesus Christ; and when the Mass was finished, then the most serene lord emperor offered gifts.[364]

The offence given to Byzantium by this act can scarcely be imagined.[365] It blew wide open the compromise which concealed the divergence between the papal and imperial conceptions of ecclesiastical *Romanitas*. Although there were some attempts to negotiate a marriage between Charlemagne and Irene, there can have been no serious idea of Charles extending his rule to encompass the Eastern empire. The *translatio imperii* implied that the office of emperor was a subordinate one in a unitary Christendom defined by obedience to the Roman pontiff, not by the sovereignty of the *Basileus ton Romaion*. This was particularly emphasized by an innovation of St Leo III's in the rite of coronation (a ceremony which had only ever been enacted up until then in Constantinople). In 800, for the first time, the pope acclaimed and crowned the imperial candidate first and only then did the people acclaim him as Augustus, giving the impression that the pope actually *conferred* the imperial dignity rather than, as the Patriarch in New Rome, merely *recognizing* it.[366]

---

[364] Louis Duchesne, ed., *Liber Pontificalis* (Paris: E. Thorin, 1886–1892) in Richard Sullivan, *The Coronation of Charlemagne* (Boston: D.C. Heath, 1959), 2.

[365] "The foundation of the Empire of Charles the Great had the same revolutionary effect in the political sphere as the later schism in the religious sphere": George Ostrogorsky, *History of the Byzantine State* (New Brunswick, NJ: Rutgers University Press, 1969), 185.

[366] King, *Charlemagne*, 41.

Charlemagne himself seems to have grasped the significance of this act and, according to Einhard, said—despite the fact that the *City of God* was his favourite book—that he would never have entered the basilica that morning if he had known what was going to happen.[367] He never returned to Rome and crowned his son with his own hand in Aachen. It was of no avail. Louis the Pious later travelled to Rome to be crowned by the pope. The principle was firmly established in the minds of Westerners that the title of Roman emperor was in the gift of the Holy See. Certainly, this act played a very significant background role in the Photian schism which erupted half a century later. Something which is missed, however, is that the creation of the new papally sponsored imperial title created a function *de jure* for the emperor in the papal concept of Roman Christendom, a function not obvious from the concept itself.

Tragically, the obvious resolution—for the emperor of New Rome to receive his diadem from the hands of the Successor of St Peter—was not pursued until the reign of Manuel I in the twelfth century, when the collapse of Byzantine power was nearly irreversible.[368] Full recognition from Rome for the Byzantine emperor would have to await the Council of Florence, and by then the empire had less than two decades of life left in it.

---

[367] Paul Edward Dutton, *Charlemagne's Courtier: The Complete Einhard* (Peterborough, ON: Broadview Press, 1998), 33.

[368] Paul Magdalino, *The Empire of Manuel I Komnenos, 1143–1180* (Cambridge: Cambridge University Press, 1993), 90.

Conclusion

Leo XIII taught that the ideal relationship between the temporal and spiritual powers resembles that between the soul and the body in man.[369] This is a thought that goes back as far as the *Epistle to Diognetus* in the second century.[370] For all that there is a perpetual conflict between the church and the world, it is the Catholic Church herself and not the unholy

[369] Leo XIII, *Immortale Dei* §14.

[370] "To put it briefly, the relation of Christians to the world is that of a soul to the body. As the soul is diffused through every part of the body, so are Christians through all the cities of the world. The soul, too, inhabits the body, while at the same time forming no part of it; and Christians inhabit the world, but they are not part of the world. The soul, invisible herself, is immured within a visible body; so Christians can be recognized in the world, but their Christianity itself remains hidden from the eye. The flesh hates the soul, and wars against her without any provocation, because she is an obstacle to its own self-indulgence; and the world similarly hates the Christians without provocation, because they are opposed to its pleasures. All the same, the soul loves the flesh and all its members, despite their hatred for her; and Christians, too, love those who hate them. The soul, shut up inside the body, nevertheless holds the body together; and though they are confined within the world as in a dungeon, it is Christians who hold the world together. The soul, which is immortal, must dwell in a mortal tabernacle; and Christians, as they sojourn for a while in the midst of corruptibility here, look for incorruptibility in the heavens. Finally, just as to be stinted of food and drink makes for the soul's improvement, so when Christians are every day subjected to ill-treatment, they increase the more in numbers. Such is the high post of duty in which God has placed them, and it is their moral duty not to shrink from it." *Epistle to Diognetus*, in Louth, *Early Christian Writings*, 127.

nation beyond her that is, as Pius XI observed,[371] the true *Civitas Humana*, and the spiritual and temporal powers ought by right to be agencies within that one society. Within that psychosomatic unity, grace and revelation are analogous to the infused virtues and the Roman civic tradition and the perennial philosophy to the acquired virtues.

Like the neophyte, the Christendom created by Constantine and Theodosius in the fourth century is a New Creation in the sense that the catechumen is reborn from the font but the habits which resembled virtues when he entered the baptistry remain, now transformed into true virtues by the infused virtues that were given with the entry of grace into the soul. This is the truth that lies behind St Cyril's remarks to the rabbis in the ninth century.

Likewise, the acquired "virtues" remain after the believer falls into mortal sin and limit the exterior delinquency of his behaviour in this state. Even separated from grace (and therefore doomed to wither), though they will not save him, these "virtues" continue to restrain for as long as they endure. Likewise, the perennial philosophy and the Roman power restrain the decline into iniquity of the former Christendom for as long as individuals and nations retain them, even after these nations are separated from the Holy See. As St John Henry Newman observed, in a passage partly quoted earlier:

> [An] objection may be made as follows: St. Paul says, "Now ye know what withholdeth, that he (Antichrist) might be revealed in his time." Here a something is mentioned as keeping back the manifestation of the enemy of truth.
>
> He proceeds: "He that now withholdeth, will withhold, until he be taken out of the way." Now this restraining power was in early times considered to be the Roman Empire, but the Roman

[371] Pius XI, *Divini Redemptoris* (1937) §7.

Empire (it is argued) has long been taken out of the way; it follows that Antichrist has long since come. In answer to this objection, I would grant that he "that withholdeth," or "hindereth," means the power of Rome, for all the ancient writers so speak of it. And I grant that as Rome, according to the prophet Daniel's vision, succeeded Greece, so Antichrist succeeds Rome, and the Second Coming succeeds Antichrist. But it does not hence follow that Antichrist is come: for it is not clear that the Roman Empire is gone. Far from it: the Roman Empire in the view of prophecy, remains even to this day. Rome had a very different fate from the other three monsters mentioned by the Prophet, as will be seen by his description of it. "Behold a fourth beast, dreadful and terrible, and strong exceedingly; and it had great iron teeth: it devoured and brake in pieces, and stamped the residue with the feet of it: and it was diverse from all the beasts that were before it, and it had ten horns." [Dan. vii. 7.] These ten horns, an Angel informed him, "are ten kings that shall rise out of this kingdom" of Rome. As, then, the ten horns belonged to the fourth beast, and were not separate from it, so the kingdoms, into which the Roman Empire was to be divided, are but the continuation and termination of that Empire itself,—which lasts on, and in some sense lives in the view of prophecy, however we decide the historical question.

Consequently, we have not yet seen the end of the Roman Empire. "That which withholdeth" still exists, up to the manifestation of its ten horns; and till it is removed, Antichrist will not come. And from the midst of those horns he will arise, as the same Prophet informs us: "I considered the horns, and behold, there came up among them another little horn; . . . and behold, in this horn were eyes like the eyes of a man, and a mouth speaking great things." Up to the time, then, when Antichrist shall actually appear, there has been and will be a continual effort to manifest him to the world

> on the part of the powers of evil. The history of the Church is the history of that long birth. "The mystery of iniquity doth already work," says St Paul. "Even now there are many Antichrists," [1 John ii. 18.] says St John,—"every spirit that confesseth not that Jesus Christ is come in the flesh, is not of God; and this is that spirit of the Antichrist, whereof ye have heard that it should come, and even now already is it in the world." [1 John iv. 3.] It has been at work ever since, from the time of the Apostles, though kept under by him that "withholdeth."
>
> At this very time there is a fierce struggle, the spirit of Antichrist attempting to rise, and the political power in those countries which are prophetically Roman, firm and vigorous in repressing it. And in fact, we actually have before our eyes, as our fathers also in the generation before us, a fierce and lawless principle everywhere at work—a spirit of rebellion against God and man, which the powers of government in each country can barely keep under with their greatest efforts. . . . [T]he present framework of society and government, as far as it is the representative of Roman powers, is that which withholdeth, and Antichrist is that which will rise when this restraint fails.

As we have seen, the idea that the Roman polity lived on in the successor states which carved up the classical empire is a distinctively Latin idea. It was important to most of the barbarian Western kings who succeeded Rome that they could claim continuity with the empire, which was seen as the repository of legitimacy. The Latin West was forced to consider this question more deeply because of the demise of the classical administrative structures in the West in the fifth century. The question came to a head in Ostrogothic Italy which was established, with imperial blessing, after the extinction of the Western imperial line. For the Byzantines, the barbarians' enthusiasm for titles and symbolic approbation from Constantinople was a tool of diplomacy to rein them in until such a time as the nations could once more be brought into proper subjection to Constantinople. For the barbarians, on the other hand, they *mattered*, and underlay a significant difference between "good" barbarians like the Ostrogoths and the Franks and persecuting Pagans and Arians like the Anglo-Saxons and the Vandals.

But this distinction also ran through the culturally Roman population left behind in the West, the "Welsh" to use the term in its original sense. The two most famous examples in the time of the Ostrogoths are Cassiodorus and Boethius. Cassiodorus saw the Ostrogothic regime as the shape of things to come and was keen to make it work and domesticate it within a Roman and Christian worldview. This task was made easier by the thirty-five-year Acacian Schism (484–519), which meant that the Catholic Romans of Italy were out of communion with the emperor in Constantinople anyway. When this was brought to an end by the emperor Justin (518–527), Boethius, despite his glittering senatorial and administrative career, was suspected by Theodoric of seeing this ideology as a stopgap pending an eventual imperial resurgence. Boethius was executed for treason, while Cassiodorus remained loyal to the Ostrogoths all the way up to the fall of Ravenna to Belisarius in 540.

Under the supervision of the triumphant imperial government in Constantinople, Cassiodorus compiled a multi-volume collection of the letters he had ghostwritten for the barbarian government in Ravenna: the *Variae*. First among these is a letter written on behalf of Theodoric to the emperor Anastasius in Constantinople. It contains a line as important in its own way as the famous *Duo Sunt* passage in Pope Gelasius's roughly contemporary letter to the same emperor.

"Theodoric"/Cassiodorus's statement—"our monarchy is an imitation of yours, the form of the good proposed, a copy of the only empire on earth"[372]—implies that the Roman polity is the ideal of the temporal

[372] "Regnum nostrum imitatio vestra est, forma boni propositi, unici exemplar imperii."

good, the *Respublica*, but that this ideal is individuated by innumerable material conditions from one time and place to another. It is hard to hear Cassiodorus's words without thinking of St Thomas's remarks in the *Commentary on the Ethics*: "All laws are framed as they are needed for the end of the state, although only one form of government is everywhere best according to nature."[373]

The fourth monarchy subsists within the spiritual unity created by the fifth, but the original temporal *Respublica*, the Byzantine Republic, retains a "primacy of honour" as the exemplar for the rest. This vision is the product of a Latin mind that had thought deeply about the nuances of St Augustine's analysis of empire in the *City of God*, of its source in the *libido dominandi*, but also its typological resemblance to Christ's universal kingdom:

> But let us avail ourselves even in these things of the kindness of God. Let us consider how great things they [the pagan Romans] despised, how great things they endured, what lusts they subdued for the sake of human glory, who merited that glory, as it were, in reward for such virtues; and let this be useful to us even in suppressing pride, so that, as that city in which it has been promised us to reign as far surpasses this one as heaven is distant from the earth, as eternal life surpasses temporal joy, solid glory empty praise, or the society of angels the society of mortals, or the glory of Him who made the sun and moon the light of the sun and moon, the citizens of so great a country may not seem to themselves to have done anything very great, if, in order to obtain it, they have done some good works or endured some evils, when those men for this terrestrial country already obtained, did such great things, suffered such great things.

[373] "Omnes enim leges ponuntur secundum quod congruit fini politiae, sed tamen sola una est optima politia secundum naturam ubicumque sit."

> And especially are all these things to be considered, because the remission of sins which collects citizens to the celestial country has something in it to which a shadowy resemblance is found in that asylum of Romulus, whither escape from the punishment of all manner of crimes congregated that multitude with which the state was to be founded.[374]

The events of Christmas Day 800 constitute the climax of the translation of the Roman polity from the temporal to the spiritual order but they also permanently problematised that inheritance. By removing the Roman dignity from its organic and natural possessors and bestowing it upon the Frankish barbarians, Leo III destroyed the solution Cassiodorus had constructed to the question of the empire's preeminence among Christian realms. Neither the Carolingian empire nor the later Germanic Reich could be plausibly presented as the universal Roman ideal. The rupturing of the continuous classical tradition and the delegitimization of the empire on the Bosphorus meant that the rediscovery of Greek would be experienced later on as a paganising "Renaissance" and a "Reformation" of rupture, and the rediscovery of Latin republicanism as a secularising Revolution. Breathing with only one lung has long-term negative consequences for health.[375]

It is often falsely imagined that the nations of the classical Roman empire were pleased to see it fall. Nothing could be further from the truth. As Augustine implies, every freeborn Roman was endowed with citizenship centuries before his time (namely, in AD 212; see p. 5). All were subject to the same laws, all considered themselves Romans. St Athanasius is the first witness to the use of the expression Romania,[376] which

[374] Augustine, *City of God*, 5.17, in *NPNF* I, vol. 2, p. 98.

[375] John Paul II, *Ut Unum Sint* (1995) §54.

[376] Kaldellis, *Romanland*.

became a standard term for the territory inhabited by these citizens. As Claudian wrote at the beginning of the fifth century, Rome "Took the conquered to her bosom, / Made mankind a single family, / Mother not mistress to the nations, / Conquering the world a second time by the bond of affection."[377] If the *Annales Cambriae* are to be believed, as Belisarius fought for the City of Rome itself in 537, Arthur lay dying in the field of Camlann. St Bede remarks of this most mysterious period in British history:

> In the meantime, in Britain, there was some respite from foreign, but not from civil war. There still remained the ruins of cities destroyed by the enemy, and abandoned; and the natives, who had escaped the enemy, now fought against each other. However, the kings, priests, private men, and the nobility, still remembering the late calamities and slaughters, in some measure kept within bounds; but when these died, and another generation succeeded, which knew nothing of those times, and was only acquainted with the present peaceable state of things, all the bonds of sincerity and justice were so entirely broken, that there was not only no trace of them remaining, but few persons seemed to be aware that such virtues had ever existed. Among other most wicked actions, not to be expressed, which their own historian, Gildas, mournfully takes notice of, they added this that they never preached the faith to the Saxons, or English, who dwelt amongst them; however, the goodness of God did not forsake His people whom He foreknew, but sent to the aforesaid nation much more worthy preachers, to bring it to the faith.[378]

---

377 John Morris, *The Age of Arthur: A History of the British Isles from 350 to 650* (New York: Barnes & Noble, 1997).

378 St Bede, *Ecclesiastical History*, Bk. I, ch. 22.

The Welsh, in other words, took the view of Boethius and the Byzantines, while God and St Gregory sided with Cassiodorus.[379]

It is remarkable that it should be Cassiodorus who stands at the head of this long tradition because he is far *more* famous for his promotion of the liberal educational tradition to which he turned once he was excluded from public life by the victorious Justinian.[380] But there is a vital connection between the cultural unity engendered by this tradition and the geopolitical unity created by the republican ideal it espouses and fosters. It is because such men are needed to maintain such structures that the institutions necessary to create them were patronised by Western governments of antiquity and the Middle Ages. Cassiodorus is the type and the model of Newman's gentleman and the embodiment of that chivalry which Burke feared dead in 1789, the bulwark of "the present framework of society and government, as far as it is the representative of Roman powers." The Hellenic educational tradition and the Roman civic tradition are inseparable:

> Now, before going on to speak of the education, and the standards of education, which the Civilized World, as I may now call it, has enjoined and requires, I wish to draw your attention, Gentlemen, to the circumstance that this same *orbis terrarum*, which has been the seat of Civilization, will be found, on the whole, to be the seat also of that supernatural society and system which our Maker has given us directly from Himself, the Christian Polity. The natural and divine associations are not indeed exactly coincident, nor ever

379 It is interesting to consider Edmund Burke's famous *Speech on Conciliation with America* (1775) in the light of Cassiodorus's vision.

380 Daniel 4:13–15: "I saw in the visions of my head as I lay in bed, and behold, a watcher, a holy one, came down from heaven. He cried aloud and said thus, 'Hew down the tree and cut off its branches, strip off its leaves and scatter its fruit; let the beasts flee from under it and the birds from its branches. But leave the stump of its roots in the earth, bound with a band of iron and bronze, amid the tender grass of the field. Let him be wet with the dew of heaven; let his lot be with the beasts in the grass of the earth.'"

> have been. As the territory of Civilization has varied with itself in different ages, while on the whole it has been the same, so, in like manner, Christianity has fallen partly outside Civilization, and Civilization partly outside Christianity; but, on the whole, the two have occupied one and the same *orbis terrarum*. Often indeed they have even moved *pari passu*, and at all times there has been found the most intimate connexion between them. Christianity waited till the *orbis terrarum* attained its most perfect form before it appeared; and it soon coalesced, and has ever since co-operated, and often seemed identical, with the Civilization which is its companion.[381]

If, then, the universal *imperium* is essentially spiritual and the Roman state persists only as an exemplar polity, it is easy to imagine that the papal vision of ecclesiastical *Romanitas* is simply correct and exhausts the doctrine, and in a sense this is true. The centrality of this concept (of a universal spiritual power) to Western culture is illustrated by the enthusiasm in the second half of the twentieth century for human rights declarations and international and supranational institutions designed to guarantee peace and human dignity, even perhaps by the contrasting enthusiasm in the first half of the twentieth century for the absolute state that enters the heart and mind and demands the whole person. From the perspective of an authentic Catholic analysis of temporal power, such institutions are absurd: towers of Babel that seek by finite effort and power to traverse the infinite.[382] As Pius XI asseverates:

> There exists an institution able to safeguard the sanctity of the law of nations. This institution is a part of every nation; at the same time it is above all nations. She enjoys, too, the highest authority,

[381] St John Henry Newman, *The Idea of a University* (London: Longmans, Green, and Co., 1907), 254–55.

[382] Pius XI, *Studiorum Ducem* (1923) §20.

> the fullness of the teaching power of the Apostles. Such an institution is the Church of Christ. She alone is adapted to do this great work, for she is not only divinely commissioned to lead mankind, but moreover, because of her very make-up and the constitution which she possesses, by reason of her age-old traditions and her great prestige, which has not been lessened but has been greatly increased since the close of the War [1914–1918], cannot but succeed in such a venture where others assuredly will fail. It is apparent from these considerations that true peace, the peace of Christ, is impossible unless we are willing and ready to accept the fundamental principles of Christianity, unless we are willing to observe the teachings and obey the law of Christ, both in public and private life. If this were done, then society being placed at last on a sound foundation, the Church would be able, in the exercise of its divinely given ministry and by means of the teaching authority which results therefrom, to protect all the rights of God over men and nations.[383]

Just as the spiritual *Romanitas* of the papacy has its modern secular imitators, so does the exemplary Byzantine republic of the *Variae*. The resemblance between the Augustan ideal set out in Question 105 of the *Prima Secundae* and the US Constitution is striking. In *Longinqua Oceani* (1895) Leo XIII famously called the USA "the well-ordered republic." As the principal factors leading to a departure from the universal abstract ideal of government are usually listed as climate and custom, it is appropriate that the USA, made up of every possible climate and a population drawn from every human culture, should preserve the universal governmental form as its own. And yet, the United States of America, which established itself by supplanting the dominions of Britain, France, and Spain, is the first Western polity since the fourth century not to profess the truth of

[383] Pius XI, *Ubi Arcano Dei Consilio* (1922) §46–47.

the Gospel as part of its public law. The stars which occupy the top left of its flag are placed there in lieu of the holy and life-giving Cross. The staff from which it hangs is surmounted by an eagle wrought of gold. In this way the "deadly wound" of the pre-Constantinian Roman empire appears to have been healed. "After the manner of the law of Augustus, by whom the empire of Rome was established,"[384] "the revolutionary doctrines of 1776 and 1789"[385] have made a place for themselves upon the earth and, as the last two centuries have proved, the ancient "framework of society and government" can restrain them no longer.

The legitimacy of political society is derived not "from the consent of the governed" but from that society's transcription and enforcement of natural law and its determination of indifferent matters whose determination (but not the manner of whose determination) is demanded by that law.[386] Enactments of the temporal power contrary to the natural law are null and void.[387] The problem of such enactments cannot be remedied by building extra storeys onto the temporal power. Only a divinely guaranteed tribunal could avert this danger, and from the nature of the case (because the natural law is by its nature the same for all men) such a tribunal ought to be universal. God has supplied such an authority in the form of the supreme magisterium of the Catholic Church. This is the kingdom of the saints of the Most High. Their kingdom is not of this world and yet it is an everlasting kingdom, and all dominions shall serve and obey it. But every court needs an officer. Should not the faithful constantly aspire to restore the Holy Empire as an essential element in the social kingship of Christ?

---

[384] Hippolytus, PG 10:768. Trans. J.H. MacMahon, in *ANF*, vol. 5 (Buffalo, NY: Christian Literature Publishing Co., 1886), 214 ; see above, p. 82.

[385] St John Henry Newman, "Liberalism," in *Apologia Pro Vita Sua* (London: Oxford University Press, 1913), 496.

[386] Leo XIII, *Libertas* §9.

[387] Leo XIII, *Diuturnum Illud* §15.

Dante proposed an absolute universal temporal monarchy, akin (one fears) to those which sought to establish themselves between 1917 and 1953.[388] In *De Ecclesiastica Potestate*, Dante's contemporary Giles of Rome considered why the pontifical authority should not simply replace that of the temporal power altogether—or, to put it another way, why social authority is bifurcated. Giles concludes[389] that it was not always thus. Originally authority in both spheres belonged to the priestly line of Adam and Noah, but first of all temporal power was usurped (Nimrod), and then the anxiety to which man is subjected by his wounded state meant that the powers had to be separated *de jure*.[390] This then is enough to demonstrate both why there must be two powers, and why, in the words of Giles's teacher St Thomas, to "the chief priest, the successor of St. Peter, the Vicar of Christ, the Roman Pontiff . . . all the kings of the Christian People are

[388] Dante, *Monarchy* (Cambridge: Cambridge University Press, 1996). See Etienne Gilson, *Dante the Philosopher* (London: Sheed and Ward, 1952).

[389] *Giles of Rome's "On Ecclesiastical Power": A Medieval Theory of World Government: A Critical Edition and Translation*, trans R.W. Dyson (New York: Columbia University Press, 2004), 277.

[390] Giles, 113. Giles cites Bede's exegesis of Luke 22:36. Bede, *In Lucae evangelium expositio 6* (PL 92:601). See also St Gelasius, *Tractate IV*, in Hugo Rahner, *Church and State in Early Christianity* (San Francisco: Ignatius Press, 1992). "For Christ, mindful of human frailty, regulated with an excellent disposition what pertained to the salvation of his people. Thus he distinguished between the offices of both powers according to their own proper activities and separate dignities, wanting his people to be saved by healthful humility and not carried away again by human pride, so that Christian emperors would need priests for attaining eternal life, and priests would avail themselves of imperial regulations in the conduct of temporal affairs. In this fashion spiritual activity would be set apart from worldly encroachments and the 'soldier of God' (2 Tim 2:4) would not be involved in secular affairs, while on the other hand he who was involved in secular affairs would not seem to preside over divine matters. Thus the humility of each order would be preserved, neither being exalted by the subservience of the other, and each profession would be especially fitted for its appropriate functions." Cf. Tierney, *Crisis of Church and State*, 13–15.

to be subject as to our Lord Jesus Christ Himself."[391] While this justifies a national temporal ruler and a distinct and higher universal spiritual power, whence arises the necessity of a highest temporal ruler? Giles's argument would seem to confirm the famous assertion of his patron Boniface VIII: "I am the emperor, I am Caesar!"[392] What need is there for the continuing office of a Roman emperor in the temporal order?

It is important not to overstate the Caesaropapism of Byzantium. In certain moments it was frank and expressed, but not usually.[393] It arose out of a certain logic. The emperor John VIII at the Council of Florence was very clear that while he could bring the bishops to make doctrinal judgments and could express his preferences, they alone could judge.[394] The central difficulty was that of disputed elections. Even before the conversion of Constantine, the pagan emperor and near-miss persecutor Aurelian had been called in by the bishops of the East to expel the deposed bishop of Antioch, Paul of Samosata. Aurelian pleasingly said he would recognize whichever bishop was recognized by the bishop of Rome.[395] In the end, though, however docile to the Holy See the temporal power may be, it has to recognize one or another occupant of a cathedral or a monastery and give effect (or not) by its corporeal might to the decrees issued by the one who wields the spiritual sword. The Faith and the Church are universal. Even papal elections are from time to time disputed and not a few emperors have intervened to eject one candidate or another. A docile and catholic (in both senses) temporal power thus remains part of the *bene esse* of the Church militant.

---

391 Aquinas, *On Kingship*, Phelan ed., 62.

392 Charles Mitchell, "The Lateran Fresco of Boniface VIII," in *Journal of the Warburg and Courtauld Institutes*, vol. 14, nos. 1/2 (1951): 1–6.

393 Gilbert Dagron, *Emperor and Priest: The Imperial Office in Byzantium* (Cambridge: Cambridge University Press, 2007).

394 Joseph Gill, *The Council of Florence* (Cambridge: Cambridge University Press, 1959), 259.

395 Eusebius of Caesarea, *History of the Church*, 7.30 (PG 20:720).

Leo X in the Bull *Exsurge Domine* of 1520 condemning the errors of Martin Luther, reflecting on the emergence of the Lutheran heresy in Germany, remarked: "We grieve the more that this happened there because we and our predecessors have always held this nation in the bosom of our affection. For after the empire had been transferred by the Roman Church from the Greeks to these same Germans, our predecessors and we always took the Church's advocates and defenders from among them."[396] And yet it is not clear that the Alps in the end proved so much more of a barrier to the temptation to usurp the spiritual sword than the Adriatic. Even after 1204, the idea of translating the papally reconceived empire back to the Greeks lingered on.[397] This idea in a certain sense defined the High Middle Ages. The papal monarchy of the eleventh to the thirteenth centuries was only possible because of the loss of the Eastern churches, but that monarchy's most distinctive activity—the Crusades—was aimed first and foremost at healing the Eastern schism. The seventeenth ecumenical council and the Crusade of Varna—which heroically sought and failed, at the cost of the king of Poland and Hungary and the Papal Legate's life, to rescue Byzantium—were the fitting but tragic climax of the *Medium Aevum*. The idea of a retranslation of empire lingers on in the elusive hope for the conversion of Russia, as Vladimir Soloviev saw as early as 1889 in his appeal to Leo XIII to crown the Tsar as Holy Roman Emperor:

> Oh deathless spirit of the blessed Apostle, invisible minister of the Lord in the government of His visible Church, thou knowest that she has need of an earthly body for her manifestation. Twice already thou hast embodied her in human society: in the Greco-Roman world, and again in the Romano-German world;

[396] Leo X, *Exsurge Domine* (1520).

[397] Nichols, *Rome and the Eastern Churches*, 186; Gill, *Byzantium and the Papacy*, 3–4.

> thou hast made both the empire of Constantine and the empire of Charlemagne to serve her. After these two provisional incarnations she awaits her third and last incarnation. A whole world full of energies and of yearnings but with no clear consciousness of its destiny knocks at the door of universal history. What is your word, ye peoples of the world? . . . Your word, O peoples of the world, is free and universal Theocracy, the true solidarity of all nations and classes, the application of Christianity to public life, the Christianising of politics; freedom for all the oppressed, protection for all the weak; social justice and good Christian peace. Open to them therefore, thou key-bearer of Christ, and may the gate of history be for them and for the whole world the gate of the Kingdom of God![398]

Eight years earlier, in his 1881 encyclical *Diuturnum Illud* on the origin of the civil power, Leo XIII taught:

> From the time when the civil society of men, raised from the ruins of the Roman Empire, gave hope of its future Christian greatness, the Roman Pontiffs, by the institution of the Holy Empire, consecrated the political power in a wonderful manner. Greatly, indeed, was the authority of rulers ennobled; and it is not to be doubted that what was then instituted would always have been a very great gain, both to ecclesiastical and civil society, if princes and peoples had ever looked to the same object as the Church. And, indeed, tranquility and a sufficient prosperity lasted so long as there was a friendly agreement between these two powers.[399]

[398] Vladimir Soloviev, *Russia and the Universal Church* (London: Geoffrey Bles, 1948), 35.

[399] Quoted from Etienne Gilson, *The Church Speaks to the Modern World* (Garden City, NY: Image Books, 1954), 150.

But the conversion of Russia remains elusive.[400] It is hard to descry such an event in the inspired narrative of Scripture or the writings of the Fathers. It is hard not to believe that the revolt "against the faith and government of the Holy Roman Church" predicted by St Thomas is well underway. If the Fathers are right in their understanding of Daniel and Revelation, we cannot now look to a revival of the Holy Empire except as the terrible instrument of the Antichrist. The first empire of Augustus served its providential purpose despite itself. The Holy Empire served out its thousand years. A third Rome is not to be sought. As Dom Prosper Guéranger lamented on the feast of St Boniface:

> At the sight of thy works, and remembering the great popes and magnificent princes, whose glory is indeed derived from thee, our admiration equals our gratitude. But pardon us, dear saint, if the thought of those grand centuries of yore, so far removed, alas, from these our days, should mingle sadness with our joy. Viewed in the light of thy holy policy and its results, O glorious precursor of the confederation of Christian nations, how we must bewail the fatal errors of those princes and statesmen, so renowned in the seventeenth century, and so foolishly admired by a world whose ruin they were hastening! For, by the isolation of Catholic nations from one another, the ties that bound them to the Vicar of Christ became loosened: princes, forgetful of their true position as representatives of the divine King, made friends with heresy, in order to assert their independence of Rome or to lower one another's power. Therefore Christendom is no more. Upon its ruins, like a woeful mimicry of the Holy Empire, Protestantism has raised its false evangelical empire, formed of nought but encroachments, and

[400] Perhaps this should not surprise us. See *Fatima in Lucia's Own Words*, ed. L. Kondor (Fatima: Secretariado dos Pastorinhos, 2007), 198.

> tracing its recognized origin to the apostasy of that felon knight Albert of Brandenburg. The complicities that rendered such a thing possible have received their chastisement. May God's justice be satisfied at last! O Boniface, cry out with us unto the God of armies for mercy. Raise up in the Church servants of Christ, powerful in word and work, as thou wast. Save France from anarchy; and restore to Germany a right appreciation of true greatness, together with the faith of her ancient days.[401]

Dom Guéranger wrote in the wake of the Franco-Prussian War and the collapse of Napoleon III's relatively pro-Catholic regime. His hopes for France and Germany would be disappointed and the Hohenzollerns would take two more rulers with them before they were done—"the Emperors Nicholas and Charles, last inheritors of the East and West Roman thrones."[402] The last inheritors: for it is not the new Rome but the New Jerusalem which will descend from heaven like a bride prepared for her husband. "The glorious Messiah's coming is suspended at every moment of history until his recognition by 'all Israel.'"[403] For, as St Paul himself warned the Romans, the covenant will return to Israel: "for if the casting away of them be the reconciling of the world, what shall the receiving of them be but life from the dead?"[404] In the interim, therefore, the papacy may have to content itself with sitting crowned upon the grave of the temporal *imperium*. And for the faithful, perhaps all we can do is "be watchful and strengthen the things that remain."[405]

---

401 Prosper Guéranger, *The Liturgical Year*, vol. 12 (Fitzwilliam, NH: Loreto Press, 2000), 84–85.

402 Robert Byron, *The Byzantine Achievement* (London: Routledge and Kegan Paul, 1987), 73.

403 CCC 674.

404 Romans 11:15.

405 Revelation 3:2.

The "servants of Christ, powerful in word and work, as thou wast" for whom Guéranger prayed may therefore have to imitate Boniface more in the ending of their earthly pilgrimage than in its course. And yet Daniel promises us that the saints of the Most High will possess the final kingdom "forever and ever." Thus, wherever that pilgrimage ends, they will be able to say with Marcus of Chesterton's *Ballad of the White Horse*:

> Lift not my head from bloody ground,
> Bear not my body home,
> For all the earth is Roman earth
> And I shall die in Rome.[406]

[406] G.K. Chesterton, *The Ballad of the White Horse* (San Francisco: Ignatius Press, 2001), 94.

Bibliography

Primary Sources

Scripture

Biblia Sacra Iuxta Vulgatam Clementinam. Edited by St Jerome. London: Baronius Press, 2003.

The Holy Bible—Douay Rheims Version. Trans. R. Challoner. London: Baronius Press, 2003.

The Holy Bible—Revised Standard Version Catholic Edition. Charlotte, NC: Saint Benedict Press, 2009.

Nova Vulgata Bibliorum Sacrorum Editio. Rome: Libreria Editrice Vaticana, 1986.

Novum Testamentum Graece et Latine. Edited by E. & E. Nestle and B. & K. Aland. Stuttgart: Deutsche Bibelgesellschaft, 2008.

Septuaginta. Edited by A. Rahlfs and R. Hanhart. Stuttgart: Deutsche Bibelgesellschaft, 2006.

Fathers

Patrologiae Cursus Completus. Series Latina [PL]. Edited by Jacques-Paul Migne. Paris, 1841–1855.

Patrologiae Cursus Completus. Series Graeca [PG]. Edited by Jacques-Paul Migne. Paris, 1857–1866.

St Ambrose. *On II Thessalonians.* PL 17.

St Augustine of Hippo. *The City of God.* Translated by M. Dods. *Nicene and Post-Nicene Fathers,* First Series, vol. 2. Buffalo, NY: Christian Literature Publishing Co., 1887.

———. *On the Free Choice of the Will.* Translated by T. Williams. Hackett: Indianapolis, 1993. See PL 32.

———. *Letters.* Translated by J.G. Cunningham. *Nicene and Post-Nicene Fathers,* First Series, vol. 1. Buffalo, NY: Christian Literature Publishing Co., 1887. See PL 33.

———. *Letters,* vol. 4. Translated by W. Parsons. New York: Fathers of the Church, 1955. See PL 33.

St Bede. *Commentary on Revelation.* Translated by F. Wallis. Liverpool: Liverpool University Press, 2013.

———. *Ecclesiastical History of the English People, with Bede's Letter to Egbert and Cuthbert's Letter on the Death of Bede.* Translated by Leo Sherley-Price. Penguin: London: 1990.

———. *In Lucae evangelium expositio.* PL 92.

———. *In Primam Epistolam Petri.* PL 93.

———. *On the Nature of Things; On Times.* Translated by C. B. Kendall and F. Wallis. Liverpool: Liverpool University Press, 2010.

———. *On the Tabernacle.* Translated by A.G. Holder. Liverpool: Liverpool University Press, 1994.

St Clement of Rome. *Letter to the Corinthians.* In *Early Christian Writings: The Apostolic Fathers,* ed. Andrew Louth. Harmondsworth, England: Penguin Books, 1987.

St Cyril of Alexandria. *A Commentary on the Gospel according to St Luke.* Translated by R. Payne Smith. Oxford: Oxford University Press, 1859.

St Cyril of Jerusalem. *Catechetical Lectures.* Translated by E. H. Gifford. *Nicene and Post-Nicene Fathers,* Second Series, vol. 7. Buffalo, NY: Christian Literature Publishing Co., 1894. See PG 33.

St Gelasius. *Duo Sunt.* PL 59.

St Gregory the Great. *Epistolae.* PL 77.

———. *Forty Gospel Homilies.* Translated by H. D. Gregory. Kalamazoo, MI: Cistercian Publications, 1990. See PL 76.

———. *The Letters of Gregory the Great.* Translated by Martyn Gregory and R. C. John. Toronto: Pontifical Institute of Mediaeval Studies, 2004.

St Hippolytus. *On Christ and Antichrist.* Translated by J.H. MacMahon. *Ante-Nicene Fathers*, vol. 5. Buffalo, NY: Christian Literature Publishing Co., 1886. See PG 10.

———. *Scholia on Daniel.* Translated by S.D.F. Salmond. *Ante-Nicene Fathers*, vol. 5. Buffalo, NY: Christian Literature Publishing Co., 1886. See PG 10.

St Ignatius of Antioch. *Letter to the Romans.* In *Early Christian Writings: The Apostolic Fathers*, ed. Andrew Louth. Harmondsworth, England: Penguin Books, 1987.

St Irenaeus. *Adversus Haereses.* Translated by A. Roberts and W. Rambaut. *Ante-Nicene Fathers*, vol. 1. Buffalo, NY: Christian Literature Publishing Co., 1885. See PG 7.

St Justin Martyr. *Dialogue with Trypho the Jew.* Translated by M. Dods and G. Reith. *Ante-Nicene Fathers*, vol. 1. Buffalo, NY: Christian Literature Publishing Co., 1885.

St Isidore of Seville. *The Etymologies.* Translated by S.A. Barney, et al. Cambridge: Cambridge University Press, 2006.

St Jerome. *Commentariorum in Isaiam Prophetam.* PL 24.

———. *Commentary on Daniel.* Translated by G.L. Archer, *Jerome's Commentary on Daniel.* Eugene, OR: Wipf & Stock, 2009. See PG 25.

———. *De Viris Illustribus.* PL 23.

———. *Epistles.* Translated by W.H. Fremantle, G. Lewis, and W.G. Martley. *Nicene and Post-Nicene Fathers*, Second Series, vol. 6. Buffalo, NY: Christian Literature Publishing Co., 1893.

St John Chrysostom. *Homilies on Romans.* Translated by J. Walker, J. Sheppard, and H. Browne. *Nicene and Post-Nicene Fathers*, First Series, vol. 11. Buffalo, NY: Christian Literature Publishing Co., 1889. See PG 62.

———. *Homilies on Second Thessalonians*. Translated by J. A. Broadus. *Nicene and Post-Nicene Fathers*, First Series, vol. 13. Buffalo, NY: Christian Literature Publishing Co., 1889. See PG 62.

St John Damascene. *The Fount of Knowledge*. Translated by Frederic H. Chase, in *Writings of St John Damascene*. Washington, DC: Catholic University of America Press, 1958.

St Leo the Great. *Letters*. Translated by Charles Lett Feltoe. *Nicene and Post-Nicene Fathers*, Second Series, vol. 12. Buffalo, NY: Christian Literature Publishing Co., 1895. See PL 54.

———. *Sermons*. Translated by Charles Lett Feltoe. *Nicene and Post-Nicene Fathers*, Second Series, vol. 12. Buffalo, NY: Christian Literature Publishing Co., 1895. See PL 54.

St Optatus of Milevis. *De Schismate Donatistarum*. PL 11.

St Patrick. *Letter to the Soldiers of Coroticus*. In *The World of St Patrick*, translated by P. Freeman. Oxford: Oxford University Press, 2014.

St Peter Chrysologus. *Selected Sermons*. Translated by George E. Ganss. Washington, DC: Catholic University of America Press, 1953.

St Severinus Boethius. *The Consolation of Philosophy*. Translated by V.E. Watts. London: Penguin, 2003.

Magisterium (by Year)

Enchiridion Symbolorum: A Compendium of Creeds, Definitions and Declarations of the Catholic Church. Edited by H. Denzinger and P. Hünermann. San Francisco: Ignatius Press, 2008.

Decrees of the Ecumenical Councils. Edited by Norman P. Tanner. London: Sheed and Ward, 1990.

The Roman Martyrology. Translated by Raphael Collins and Joseph B. Collins. Fitzwilliam, NH: Loreto, 2000.

First Ecumenical Council of Nicaea (325).

Boniface VIII. *Unam Sanctam* (1302).

Ecumenical Council of Vienne (1311–1312).

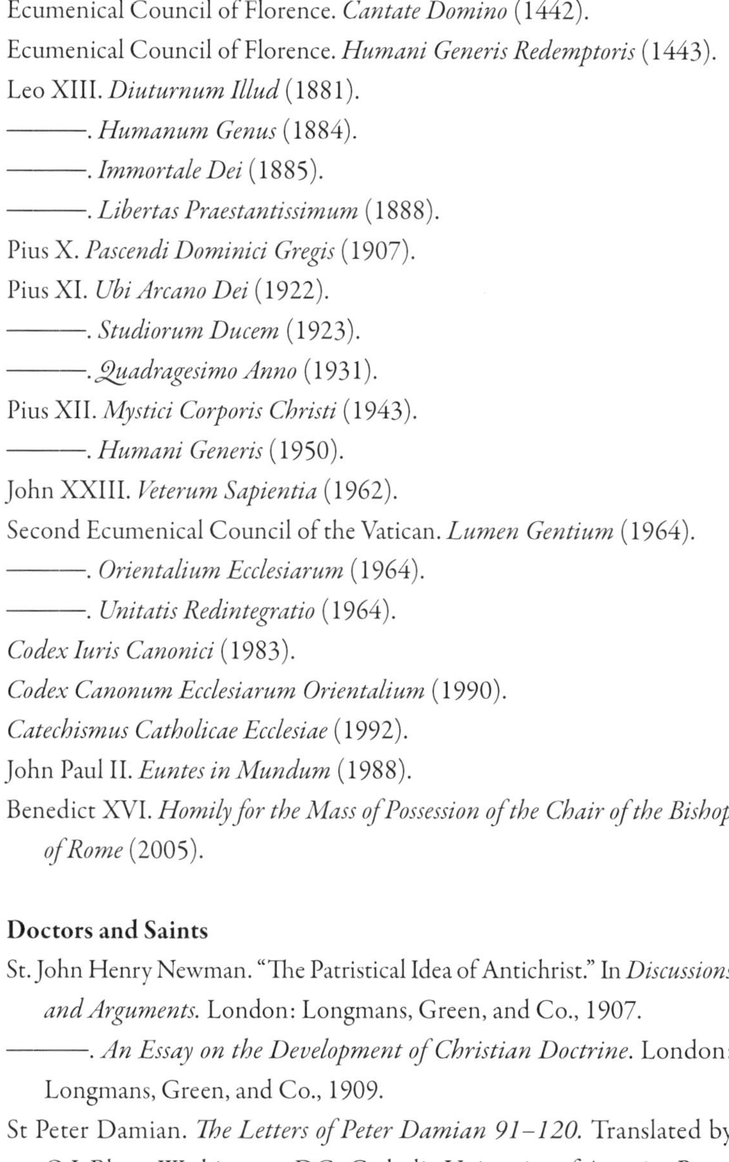

Ecumenical Council of Florence. *Cantate Domino* (1442).

Ecumenical Council of Florence. *Humani Generis Redemptoris* (1443).

Leo XIII. *Diuturnum Illud* (1881).

———. *Humanum Genus* (1884).

———. *Immortale Dei* (1885).

———. *Libertas Praestantissimum* (1888).

Pius X. *Pascendi Dominici Gregis* (1907).

Pius XI. *Ubi Arcano Dei* (1922).

———. *Studiorum Ducem* (1923).

———. *Quadragesimo Anno* (1931).

Pius XII. *Mystici Corporis Christi* (1943).

———. *Humani Generis* (1950).

John XXIII. *Veterum Sapientia* (1962).

Second Ecumenical Council of the Vatican. *Lumen Gentium* (1964).

———. *Orientalium Ecclesiarum* (1964).

———. *Unitatis Redintegratio* (1964).

Codex Iuris Canonici (1983).

Codex Canonum Ecclesiarum Orientalium (1990).

Catechismus Catholicae Ecclesiae (1992).

John Paul II. *Euntes in Mundum* (1988).

Benedict XVI. *Homily for the Mass of Possession of the Chair of the Bishop of Rome* (2005).

Doctors and Saints

St. John Henry Newman. "The Patristical Idea of Antichrist." In *Discussions and Arguments*. London: Longmans, Green, and Co., 1907.

———. *An Essay on the Development of Christian Doctrine*. London: Longmans, Green, and Co., 1909.

St Peter Damian. *The Letters of Peter Damian 91–120*. Translated by O.J. Blum. Washington, DC: Catholic University of America Press, 1998.

———. *The Letters of Peter Damian 121–150.* Translated by O.J. Blum. Washington, DC: Catholic University of America Press, 2004.

St Thomas Aquinas. *Commentary on the Letters of St Paul to the Philippians, Colossians, Thessalonians, Timothy, Titus, and Philemon.* Lander, WY: Aquinas Institute, 2012.

———. *Commentary on the Gospel of Matthew, Chapters 13–28.* Lander, WY: Aquinas Institute, 2013.

———. *On Kingship: To the King of Cyprus.* Translated Gerald B. Phelan. Toronto: Pontifical Institute of Mediaeval Studies, 1982.

———. *Summa theologiae.* Madrid: Biblioteca de Autores Cristianos, 1955.

———. *Summa Theologica.* Translated by Fathers of the English Dominican Province. New York: Benziger Brothers, 1947.

———. *De Veritate, Questions 10–20.* Translated James V. McGlynn. Chicago: Henry Regnery Company, 1953.

Other Ancient and Mediaeval Authors

Anonymous. *The Letter of Barnabas.* In *Early Christian Writings: The Apostolic Fathers*, translated by Andrew Louth. Harmondsworth: Penguin Books, 1987.

———. "Donatio Constantini." In Brian Tierney, *The Crisis of Church and State 1050–1300.* Toronto: University of Toronto Press, 2009.

———. "Life of Constantine the Philosopher." In Marvin Kantor, *Medieval Slavic Lives of Saints and Princes.* Michigan Slavic Publications. Ann Arbor, MI: The University of Michigan, 1983.

———. *The Book of the Popes (Liber Pontificalis).* Translated by L.R. Loomis. New York: Columbia University Press, 1916.

Alcuin. *Alcuin of York.* Translated by S. Allot. York: Ebor Press, 1974.

Andrew of Caesarea. *Commentary on the Apocalypse.* Translated by E.S. Constantinou. Washington, DC: Catholic University of America Press, 2011.

Ammianus Marcellinus. *Ammianus Marcellinus.* Translated by J.C. Rolfe. Cambridge, MA: Harvard University Press, 1935.

Augustus, Gaius Iulius Caesar Octavianus. *Res gestae divi Augusti: Text, Translation, and Commentary.* Translated by Alison Cooley. Cambridge: Cambridge University Press, 2009.

Arrian. *The Campaigns of Alexander.* Harmondsworth: Penguin Books, 1971.

Aristotle. *Politics.* Mineola, NY: Dover Publications, 2000.

Cassius Dio. *The Roman History: The Reign of Augustus.* Translated by I. Scott-Kilvert. Harmondsworth: Penguin Books, 1987.

Cicero, Marcus Tullius. *De Re Publica, De Legibus.* Edited by Clinton Walker Keyes. Cambridge, MA: Harvard University Press, 2006.

———. *The Republic and the Laws.* Oxford: Oxford World's Classics, 1998.

Constantinus, Flavius Valerius. *Oratio ad sanctorum coetum.* PL 8.

Cosmas Indicopleustes. *The Christian Topography of Cosmas, an Egyptian Monk: Translated from the Greek, and Edited with Notes and Introduction* by J.W. McCrindle. Cambridge: Cambridge University Press, 2010.

Dante Alighieri. *The Divine Comedy / La Divina Commedia.* Translated by Henry Wadsworth Longfellow. Oxford: Benediction Classics, 2012.

———. *Monarchy.* Cambridge: Cambridge University Press, 1996.

Einhard. *Life of Charlemagne.* In *Charlemagne's Courtier: The Complete Einhard,* translated by P. E. Dutton. Peterborough ON: Broadview Press, 1998.

Eutropius. *Breviarium Historiae Romanae.* Translated by H.W. Bird. Liverpool: Liverpool University Press, 1993.

Eusebius of Caesarea. *Church History.* Translated by Arthur Cushman McGiffert. *Nicene and Post-Nicene Fathers,* Second Series, vol. 1. Grand Rapids, MI: William B. Eerdmans, 1955.

———. *De Laudibus Constantini* and *De Vita Constantini.* Translated by E.C. Richardson. *Nicene and Post-Nicene Fathers,* Second Series, vol. 1. Buffalo, NY: Christian Literature Publishing Co., 1890. See PG 20.

———. *The History of the Church.* Translated by G.A. Williamson. London: Penguin, 1989. See PG 5.

Giles of Rome. *De Ecclesiastica Potestate.* In *Giles of Rome's "On Ecclesiastical Power": A Medieval Theory of World Government: A Critical Edition and Translation*. Translated by R. W Dyson. New York: Columbia University Press, 2004.

Iosephus, Flavius. *Josephus: The Complete Works.* Translated by William Whiston. Nashville, TN: Thomas Nelson Publishers, 2003.

Jacobus de Voragine. *The Golden Legend: Readings on the Saints.* Princeton: Princeton University Press, 2012.

Kydones, Demetrios. *Apology for his Conversion.* In James Likoudis, *Ending the Byzantine Greek Schism*. New Rochelle, NY: Catholics United for the Faith, 1992.

———. *Oratio pro subsido latinorum*. PG 154.

Lactantius. *Divine Institutes.* Translated by W. Fletcher. *Ante-Nicene Fathers*, vol. 7. Buffalo, NY: Christian Literature Publishing Co., 1886. See PL 6.

Origen. *Contra Celsum*. PG 11.

———. *On Principles.* Translated by F. Crombie. *Ante-Nicene Fathers*, vol. 4. Buffalo, NY: Christian Literature Publishing Co., 1885. See PG 11.

Philo. *Philo*, vol. 10. Translated by Francis Henry Colson. Cambridge, MA: Harvard University Press, 1962.

Photios. *The Library of Photius.* Translated by J.H. Freese. New York: MacMillan, 1920. See PG 103.

Pius II. *Commentaries*, vol. 1. Edited by Margaret Meserve and Marcello Simonetta. London: Harvard University Press, 2003.

Polybius. *The Rise of the Roman Empire.* Translated by I. Scott-Kilvert. London: Penguin, 1979.

Prudentius. *Prudentius*, vol. 2. Translated by H.J. Thomson. Cambridge: Harvard University Press, 1949.

Suetonius. *Lives of the Caesars.* Translated by J.C. Rolfe. Cambridge: Harvard University Press, 1997.

Sextus Aurelius Victor. *De Caesaribus.* Translated by H.W. Bird. Liverpool: Liverpool University Press, 1994.

Tacitus. *The Complete Works of Tacitus.* Translated by Alfred John William Church, et al. New York: Modern Library, 1942.

Tertullian. *Apology*. Translated by S. Thelwall. *Ante-Nicene Fathers*, vol. 3. Buffalo, NY: Christian Literature Publishing Co., 1885.

Tertullian. *De Pudicitia*. PL 2.

Tertullian. *De Pallio*. PL 2.

Tertullian. *On the Resurrection*. Translated by P. Holmes. *Ante-Nicene Fathers*, vol. 3. Buffalo, NY: Christian Literature Publishing Co., 1885. See PL 2.

Virgil. *Eclogues. Georgics. Aeneid: Books 1–6.* Translated by H. R. Fairclough. Cambridge, MA: Harvard University Press, 1999.

Secondary Material

Books

Arminjon, Charles. *The End of the Present World and the Mysteries of Future Life*. Manchester, NH: Sophia Institute Press, 2008.

Barber, Malcolm. *Two Cities: Medieval Europe, 1050–1320*. London: Routledge, 2004.

Barber, Michael Patrick. *Coming Soon: Unlocking the Book of Revelation and Applying Its Lessons Today*. Steubenville, OH: Emmaus Road, 2005.

Barnett, Paul. *Jesus and the Rise of Early Christianity: A History of New Testament Times*. Downers Grove, IL: InterVarsity Press, 1999.

Bauckham, Richard. *The Climax of Prophecy*. London: T&T Clark, 1993.

Baynes, Norman H. *Byzantine Studies and Other Essays*. London: Athlone Press, 1955.

Belloc, Hilaire. *Europe and the Faith*. London: Burns and Oates, 1962.

Benedict XVI. *Jesus of Nazareth. Holy Week: From the Entrance into Jerusalem to the Resurrection.* San Francisco: Ignatius Press, 2011.

Braverman, J. *Jerome's Commentary on Daniel: A Study of Comparative Jewish and Christian Interpretations of the Hebrew Bible*. Washington, DC: Catholic Biblical Association of America, 1978.

Brown, Peter. *Augustine of Hippo.* London: Faber and Faber, 1967.

van Bruggen, Jakob. *Christ on Earth: The Gospel Narratives as History*. (Grand Rapids, MI: Baker Books, 1998).

Bryce, James. *The Holy Roman Empire*. London: MacMillan, 1895.

Buckland, W. W. and Arnold Duncan McNair. *Roman Law and Common Law: A Comparison in Outline*. Cambridge: Cambridge University Press, 2008.

Bullough, D. A. *Carolingian Renewal Sources and Heritage*. Manchester: Manchester University Press 1991.

Byron, Robert. *The Byzantine Achievement*. London: Routledge and Kegan Paul, 1987.

Cameron, Averil. *The Later Roman Empire, AD 284–430*. Cambridge, MA: Harvard University Press, 1993.

Chesterton, G.K. *The Ballad of the White Horse*. San Francisco: Ignatius Press, 2001.

Chilton, David. *The Days of Vengeance.* Fort Worth, TX: Dominion Press, 1987.

Collins, Roger. *Charlemagne*. Toronto: University of Toronto Press, 1998.

Congar, Yves. *After Nine Hundred Years: The Background of the Schism between the Eastern and Western Churches*. New York: Fordham University Press, 1959.

Dagron, Gilbert. *Emperor and Priest: The Imperial Office in Byzantium.* Cambridge: Cambridge University Press, 2007.

Dancy, J. C. *A Commentary on I Maccabees*. Oxford: Basil Blackwell, 1954.

Dawson, Christopher. *The Making of Europe*. London: Sheed and Ward, 1932.

Davies, W. D. and Louis Finkelstein. *The Cambridge History of Judaism.* Cambridge: Cambridge University Press, 1989.

DePalma Digeser, Elizabeth. *The Making of a Christian Empire: Lactantius and Rome*. Ithaca, NY: Cornell University Press, 2000.

DeGregorio, Scott, ed. *The Cambridge Companion to Bede*. Cambridge: Cambridge University Press, 2010.

Dutton, Paul Edward, ed. *Carolingian Civilization*. Peterborough, ON: Broadview, 1993.

Dvornik, Francis. *The Idea of Apostolicity in Byzantium and the Legend of the Apostle Andrew*. Dumbarton Oaks Studies. Cambridge, MA: Harvard University Press, 1958.

———. *The Photian Schism: History and Legend*. Cambridge: Cambridge University Press, 2008.

Foltz, Robert. *The Concept of Empire in Western Europe from the Fifth to the Fourteenth Century*. London: Edward Arnold, 1969.

———. *The Coronation of Charlemagne, 25 December 800*. London: Routledge and Kegan Paul, 1974.

Ford, Henry Jones. *Representative Government*. New York: H. Holt and Company, 1924.

Fortescue, Adrian. *The Mass: A Study of the Roman Liturgy*. Fitzwilliam, NH: Loreto Publications, 2005.

———. *The Orthodox Eastern Church*. Reprint edition. Piscataway, N.J.: Gorgias Press, 2001.

———. *The Uniate Eastern Churches*. Reprint edition. Piscataway, NJ: Gorgias Press, 2001.

Gibbon, Edward. *The Decline and Fall of the Roman Empire*. London: Everyman, 1993.

Gill, Joseph. *Byzantium and the Papacy, 1198–1400*. New Brunswick, NJ: Rutgers University Press, 1979.

———. *The Council of Florence*. Cambridge: Cambridge University Press, 1959.

Gilson, Étienne. *The Church Speaks to the Modern World*. Garden City, NY: Image Books, 1954.

———. *Dante the Philosopher*. London: Sheed and Ward, 1952.

———. *Les métamorphoses de la cité de Dieu*. Paris: J. Vrin, 2005.

Goldstein, Jonathan A. *I Maccabees*. New York: Doubleday, 1976.

Gordon, Colin D. *The Age of Attila: Fifth-Century Byzantium and the Barbarians*. Ann Arbor, MI: University of Michigan Press, 2013.

Guéranger, Prosper. *The Liturgical Year*, vol. 12. Fitzwilliam, NH: Loreto Publications, 2000.

Hartman, Louis F., and Alexander A. Di Lella. *The Book of Daniel*. New York: Doubleday, 2005.

Hayek, Friedrich A. *The Constitution of Liberty: The Definitive Edition*. Chicago: University of Chicago Press, 2011.

Heather, Peter. *The Fall of the Roman Empire a New History of Rome and the Barbarians*. Oxford: Oxford University Press, 2006.

———. *The Restoration of Rome: Barbarian Popes and Imperial Pretenders*. London: MacMillan, 2013.

Himka, John-Paul. *Religion and Nationality in Western Ukraine: The Greek Catholic Church and the Ruthenian National Movement in Galicia, 1870–1900*. Montreal: McGill-Queen's University Press, 1999.

Hobbes, Thomas. *Leviathan*. Oxford: Oxford World's Classics, 2008.

Howgego, Christopher, Volker Heuchert, and Andrew Burnett, eds. *Coinage and Identity in the Roman Provinces*. Oxford: Oxford University Press, 2005.

John Paul II. *Man and Woman He Created Them: A Theology of the Body*. Translated by Michael Waldstein. Boston, MA: Pauline Books and Media, 2006.

Kaldellis, Anthony. *Romanland: Ethnicity and Empire in Byzantium*. Cambridge, MA: Harvard University Press, 2019.

Kelly, J.N.D. *Golden Mouth: The Story of John Chrysostom—Ascetic, Preacher, Bishop*. Ithaca, NY: Cornell University Press, 1995.

King, P.D. *Charlemagne*. London: Routledge, 1986.

King, Peter. *Western Monasticism*. Kalamazoo: Cistercian Publications, 1999.

Kovacs, Judith and Christopher Rowland. *Revelation: The Apocalypse of Jesus Christ*. Oxford: Blackwell, 2004.

Lee, Alexander. *Humanism and Empire—The Imperial Idea in Fourteenth-Century Italy*. Oxford: Oxford University Press, 2018.

Lee, Samuel. *Eusebius of Caesarea. The Theophania or Divine Manifestation of Our Lord and Saviour Jesus Christ.* Cambridge: Cambridge University Press, 1843.

Lintott, Andrew. *The Constitution of the Roman Republic*. Oxford: Oxford University Press, 1999.

Louth, Andrew. *St. John Damascene: Tradition and Originality in Byzantine Theology*. Oxford: Oxford University Press, 2002.

Magdalino, Paul. *The Empire of Manuel I Komnenos, 1143–1180*. Cambridge: Cambridge University Press, 1993.

Mango, Cyril. *The Oxford History of Byzantium*. Oxford: Oxford University Press, 2002.

Mousourakis, George. *A Legal History of Rome*. Abingdon: Routledge, 2007.

Nichols, Aidan. *Rome and the Eastern Churches: A Study in Schism*. San Francisco: Ignatius Press, 2010.

Norton, Peter. *Episcopal Elections 250–600: Hierarchy and Popular Will in Late Antiquity*. Oxford: Oxford University Press, 2007.

Obolensky, Dimitri. *The Byzantine Commonwealth: Eastern Europe, 500–1453*. London: Sphere Books, 1974.

Orchard, Bernard, Edmund F. Sutcliffe, Reginald C. Fuller; Ralph Russell. *A Catholic Commentary on Holy Scripture*. London: Thomas Nelson and Sons, 1953.

Ostrogorsky, George. *History of the Byzantine State*. New Brunswick, NJ: Rutgers University Press, 1969.

Quasten, J. *Patrology*. Notre Dame IN: Christian Classics, 2000.

Rowland, Christopher. *Christian Origins: An Account of the Setting and Character of the Most Important Messianic Sect of Judaism*. London: SPCK, 1985.

Schoeman, Roy H. *Salvation is from the Jews*. San Francisco: Ignatius Press, 2003.

Shepard, Jonathan. *The Cambridge History of the Byzantine Empire c. 500–1492*. Cambridge: Cambridge University Press, 2008.

Snead-Cox, J.G. *The Life of Cardinal Vaughan*. London: Herbert and Daniel, 1910.

Spinka, Matthew, ed. *Advocates of Reform: From Wyclif to Erasmus*. Louisville, KY: Westminster Press, 1953.

Sullivan, Richard. *The Coronation of Charlemagne*. Boston: D.C. Heath, 1959.

Syme, Ronald. *The Roman Revolution*. Oxford: Oxford University Press, 2002.

Tierney, Brian. *The Crisis of Church and State 1050–1300*. Toronto: University of Toronto Press, 2009.

Ussher, James. *Annales Veteris Testamenti, a prima mundi origine deducti una cum rerum asiaticarum et aegyptiacarum chronico, a temporis historici principio usque ad . . . / Jacobo Usserio Armachano digestore*. London: E. Tyler, 1658.

Wallace-Hadrill, J.M. *The Barbarian West 400–1000*. Oxford: Blackwell, 1985.

Ward-Perkins, Bryan. *The Fall of Rome and the End of Civilization*. Oxford: Oxford University Press, 2006.

Ware, Kallistos. *The Orthodox Church*. London: Penguin Books, 1993.

Wilks, M.J. *The Problem of Sovereignty in the Late Middle Ages*. Cambridge: Cambridge University Press, 1963.

Wormald, Patrick. *The Making of English Law: King Alfred to the Twelfth Century*. Oxford: Blackwell Publishers, 1999.

Articles

Chrysos, Evangelos K. "The Title ΒΑΣΙΛΕΥΣ in Early Byzantine International Relations." *Dumbarton Oaks Papers* (1978): 29–75.

Chroust, Anton-Hermann. "The Philosophy of Law in St Augustine." *The Philosophical Review*, vol. 53, no. 2 (March 1944): 195–202.

Corbishley, Thomas. "1 and 2 Maccabees." In *A Catholic Commentary on Holy Scripture*, ed. B. Orchard, et al. London: Nelson, 1953.

Deutsch, Monroe E. "I am Caesar not Rex." *Classical Philology*, vol. 23, no. 4 (October 1928): 394–98.

Edwards, Mark. "The Beginnings of Christianisation." In *The Cambridge Companion to the Age of Constantine*, ed. N. Lenski. Cambridge: Cambridge University Press, 2012.

Erskine, Andrew. "Hellenistic Monarchy and Roman Political Invective." *The Classical Quarterly* New Series, vol. 41, no. 1 (1991): 106–20.

Kazhdan, Alexander P. "Hellenes." In *The Oxford Dictionary of Byzantium*, vol. 2. Oxford: Oxford University Press, 1991.

Keresztes, Paul. "The *Constitutio Antoniniana* and the Persecutions under Caracalla." *The American Journal of Philology*, vol. 91, no. 4 (October 1970): 446–59.

Landes, Richard. "Lest the Millennium Be Fulfilled: Apocalyptic Expectations and the Pattern of Western Chronography 100–800." In *The Use and Abuse of Eschatology in the Middle Ages*, ed. Werner Verbeke, Daniel Verhelst, and Andries Welkenhuysen. Leuven: Leuven University Press, 1988.

Mitchell, Charles. "The Lateran Fresco of Boniface VIII." *Journal of the Warburg and Courtauld Institutes*, vol. 14, no. 1/2 (1951): 1–6.

Peterson, Erik. "Monotheism as a Political Problem." In idem, *Theological Tractates*, 68–105. Stanford, CA: Stanford University Press, 2011.

Pink, Thomas. "The Interpretation of *Dignitatis Humanae*: A Reply to Martin Rhonheimer." *Nova et Vetera*, vol. 11, no. 1 (Winter 2013): 77–121.

Richards, G.C. "Proskynesis." *The Classical Review*, vol. 48, no. 5 (November 1934): 168–70.

Thurston, Herbert. "Roman Catholic." In *The Catholic Encyclopedia*. New York: Robert Appleton Company, 1912.

Tierney, Brian. "Freedom and the Medieval Church." In *The Origins of Modern Freedom in the West*, ed. Richard W. Davis. Stanford, CA: Stanford University Press, 1995.

Index of Proper Names

About the Author

Alan Fimister is Assistant Professor of Dogmatic Theology and Director of Graduate Theology at Holy Apostles College and Seminary in Connecticut. He is the author of *Robert Schuman: Neo-Scholastic Humanism and the Reunification of Europe* (2008) and, with Fr Thomas Crean O.P., *Integralism: A Manual of Political Philosophy* (2020). He is the Director of the Dialogos Institute. A native of Newcastle upon Tyne, he is married and has three children.

You might enjoy some other titles published by Os Justi Press:

Dogmatic Theology

Lattey (ed.), *The Incarnation*

Lattey (ed.), *St Thomas Aquinas*

Pohle, *God: His Knowability, Essence, and Attributes*

Pohle, *The Author of Nature and the Supernatural*

Scheeben, *A Manual of Catholic Theology* (2 vols.)

Scheeben, *Nature and Grace*

Spiritual Theology

Doyle, *Vocations*

Guardini, *Sacred Signs*

Leen, *The True Vine and Its Branches*

Swizdor, *God in Me*

Liturgy

A Benedictine Martyrology

The Life of Worship

The Roman Martyrology (Pocket Edition)

Chaignon, *The Sacrifice of the Mass Worthily Offered*

Croegaert, *The Mass: A Liturgical Commentary* (2 vols.)

Kwasniewski (ed.), *John Henry Newman on Worship, Reverence, and Ritual*

Parsch, *The Breviary Explained*

Pothier, *Cantus Mariales*

Shaw, *Sacred and Great*

Language & Literature

The Little Flowers of Saint Francis (illustrated)

Brittain, *Latin in Church*

Farrow, *Pageant of the Popes*

Kilmer, *Anthology of Catholic Poets*

Lazu Kmita, *The Island Without Seasons*

Papini, *Gog*

Walsh, *The Catholic Anthology*

Made in United States
Troutdale, OR
10/15/2023

13756117R00123